THROUGH DIFFERENT EYES

A JOSEPH A FORAN HIGH SCHOOL PUBLICATION

ISBN: 978-1-4834-6967-6 (sc)
ISBN: 978-1-4834-6966-9 (e)

Lulu Publishing Services rev. date: 5/8/2017

Contents

Cover Illustration by Nicole Eschweiler

Photograph by: Gino Esposito

About the Book

During the 2015-2016 school year, students from Joseph A. Foran High School were awarded a grant to publish a book and took part in the pilot class, Advanced Creative Writing. Through the vision of student authors and visual art students that year, Foran's first anthology, <u>Foreign Visions</u>, was published. Through the marketing and sales of their book, the success found by those students paved the way, and provided funding, for this year's book, <u>Through Different Eyes</u>.

Throughout the course of the 2016-2017 school year, students worked on various types of writing, spanning a plethora of genres, all sharing the common goal of becoming better writers. In Foran High School's second anthology, 15 young authors have come together, along with students from advanced art and photography classes, to create the second installment of a Foran anthology.

La Fábrica

They burned. My eyes, red and puffy, stung as a chemical tear ran down my cheek. Reaching up my arms in an attempt to wipe away the powdery film that had accumulated, I felt the sweat from my skin exacerbate the pain. Gritting my teeth, I blinked rapidly to quell the flames on my face. The fire was so intense that the fabric in front of me had practically lost its meaning.

My stinging eyes met the sight I hated most: the steel door, standing six feet tall, looming over me. Three inches of thick, solid metal. Details once bolted down with silver screws were now coated in rust. Remnants of tape clung to the door. A small light kept a watchful, yet ominous, eye on my work. Where the handle had been was now just another piece of welded metal. Bulky padlocks fastened on the opposite side ensured my dreams of escape would never become a reality.

My mind snapped to attention with a sudden stabbing pain in my fingertip. My hand recoiled instantly in an attempt to stop the bleeding. The too-familiar pin prick made a perfect circle in the center of my index finger.

"Mariana, tienes un vendaje?" I whispered behind me.

"Lo siento, María. I used my last one yesterday," she muttered back, keeping the focus on her garment rather than my plea for help.

"No talking, ladies! You know the rules!" Mark screeched from the back of the room, finishing his sentence with a strained cough.

With a sigh, I turned back to my desk and wrapped a scrap of fabric around my finger to stop the bleeding, watching the red stain still growing. My watch revealed that the time was barely eight. *One more hour. One more hour.* My tired mind chanted these words so much that they'd often lose their meaning.

As I heard the sound of heavy breaths behind my back, my peaceful thoughts halted. Noticing the suffocating scent of cheap cologne and stale coffee becoming stronger, I sat up straighter, keeping my eyes low.

"How many today?" he barked at me, walking around to the front of my table. He slammed his hot coffee on my already weak desk, which let out a groan in distress as liquid spilt on its withered top. I rushed to gather my neatly folded pieces out of the puddle that was spreading.

"Twelve full skirts, sir," I responded, shoving another piece of fabric into the machine. His brow furled as he grabbed one for inspection; his hands traced the seams, searching for any loose thread or imperfection on which to reprimand me.

"Hmph," he snorted as he threw it back down, unable to find any imperfection, and continued on his rounds. His leather shoes, slowly leaving my periphery, squeaked obnoxiously before stopping at Mariana's station. With a subtle eye roll, I continued sewing. Twelve skirts today would make about nineteen dollars, if he was feeling generous. His demeanor changed so rapidly that it was hard to predict. Some days he'd be on a high of stale coffee and menthol cigarettes; on others, he'd come in still grumbling about the girlfriend who left him eight months ago. On those happy days, I'd usually collect nineteen dollars, barely enough to cover the already dirt-cheap rent of my one-bedroom apartment. On the not so lucky days, I was lucky to get a five dollar bill and the change between the seats of the bus on the way home.

"Eight skirts? You have the nerve to tell me that you have made *eight* skirts today?" Mark's voice grew in volume with each word, finally booming in the background. My shoulders tensed as I waited for what was coming next. The sound of his hand hitting her face echoed through the whole factory. I froze, fabric still in hand, as the sharp sound of the impact rung overhead. A thin line of chills rolled down my spine, my eyes contracting shut in an effort to shield themselves from the damage. The constant sound of frantic sewing machines halted.

"I'm sorry, sir," Mariana whispered quietly.

"Fix it!" he yelled. "This is *two* days in a row that you haven't met

2

quota. Don't even ask for your pay tonight." She opened her mouth to plead, but the words in English simply weren't there. Her speech came out in short babbles while tears streamed down her face, her shoulders shaking as her body convulsed with sobs.

"My son," she choked out. "My son, he needs the daycare money today and-"

"*My son, my son,*" Mark mocked, rolling his eyes. "I don't wanna hear it. Keep it up and you won't have any job," he scoffed. "Be grateful I gave you anything when you can't even write your own name!" he said, laughing while pulling out another cigarette with shaking hands.

From the dim flame of his cheap lighter, his eyes lit up with a maniacal glow. He took one long drag before blowing a mouthful of smoke into Mariana's tear-streaked face. His spastic chuckles could be heard even after he had disappeared through the back door marked 'Authorized Personnel Only'.

Now the only audible sounds in the otherwise silent room were Mariana's choked back whimpers, which could be heard even through the muffling hands that covered her face in an attempt to hide her distress. My legs urged me to stand up, push out of my chair, and run to comfort her, but the popping of locks from the despised door signaled the freedom from another ten hour working day. Its huge metal door swung open, creating a brisk breeze that cooled my still scorching face. Feeling the fresh air filling my coated lungs, I shook off the sight of Mariana in anguish and grabbed my coat off the back of my chair to collect my pay.

Apartment 360. I jabbed my key into the wobbling door handle and jiggled it until it heaved open with a groan of exhaustion. My sore body was relieved to collapse on the half-sunken couch cushions. As I laid back, I reached into my coat pocket to pull out my whopping pay. The thin bills, ripped in the corners, glowed neon green in the lamp's yellow light.

"Mamá, you're home!" Luis's tiny frame stood in the hallway as he peeped out into the living room. His smiling face and chubby cheeks reminded me too much of Mariana's son tonight.

"Ay, mijo. Why are you still up?" I asked, shoving the cash back into my pocket quickly.

"Did you get your pay, Mamá? So I can go on the school trip?" he asked, eyes widening as he ran over to greet me. Instantly, my heart dropped as I heard those dreaded words come out of his mouth. It seemed that each month was another trip I could never afford to send him on. The aquarium, the science center, and the planetarium had all come and gone before I could even begin saving. The worst part was telling Luis- each month, he'd come home with another permission slip and the naïve hope that this month would be different. Yet, his reaction to hearing the bad news was always the same; the look of disappointment and teary eyes of my son always hit me like a punch in the stomach. My hands clenched at the bills in my coat pocket before I glanced up to meet his innocent face, still anticipating my response.

"How much was it again, mijo?" I asked, jangling the pocket change against my dry palms.

"Only fifty dollars, Mamá. And I'll pay you back. I promise," he beamed.

Fifty dollars? After rent? And food for the week? Looking into his hopeful eyes, my heart sunk in realization that I would soon be snuffing out his joy like an old cigarette butt.

"We'll see, love," I finally said, unable to tell him the truth.

"You said that last week! You told me you'd know today!" he cried, now with a trembling lip.

"I know, I know. Please, love. Go to bed and we'll talk tomorrow," I pleaded. Reaching out to wipe the tear in the corner of his eye, I watched him pull away with a pitiful frown before shuffling back to his room. "Te amo," I called over my shoulder, but my words were only met with the response of his door slamming shut. Trying to shake off the guilt, I stood and headed to the kitchen. Stacks of dirty paper plates were piled in the cracked sink. A half-eaten apple sat on the counter with gnats hovering around it. In the hutch, I opened the top drawer and rested the day's pay on the pitiful stack inside. My hands in the dim lights revealed several new calluses on my palms and the half-healed pinprick from earlier. My neck craned up so I could see my face in the grimy mirror fixed to the wall. The handprint that had been etched on my own face

4

for the past week was fading, but the red outline was still too visible to be forgotten. My ears still rang with the sound of the slap while my mind, already tense, couldn't shake the pained expression on Mariana's face from earlier. How could I have left her, sobbing in her plastic chair? If I hadn't done anything to stop it, I had done much worse: I had condoned it. I might as well have been just as bad as Mark himself. Grabbing two Tylenols to calm my constant headache, I trudged to the couch once more, a heavy blanket of guilt shrouding my weary shoulders. I drifted asleep to the same rerun of a telenovela that I never quite knew the name of, but watched every night.

"Mamá, good bye! I'll see you tonight!"

Still in a hazy state, I peeled open my eyelids to see Luis running out the door, his right shoelace untied as always.

"Good bye, mijo!" I called; but he was already gone, leaving the door half open and the kitchen light on. The alarm clock on the television stand read 8:23, leaving me with seven minutes to clean myself up before catching the bus. Despite a few stains on my shirt, the clothes from yesterday would suffice as an outfit for the day. My body snapped to attention before my mind could catch up; running frantically around the kitchen, I swiped a messy coat of ninety-nine cent lipstick on my chapped mouth and grabbed my bag before shutting the light and slamming the door behind me. My watch now revealed the dreaded sight of 8:29, sending my feet into a flurry down the steep stairs. By the time I pushed through the final door and out into the street, the bus was closing its doors.

"Wait, wait!" I yelled, tripping over the uneven sidewalk. The shrill squeaking of the reluctant driver cranking the doors open again meant I would make rent for another week. "Thank you, thank you," I panted, crumpling into the empty seat next to Luana.

"Buenos días, María," she muttered, biting her nails. Her brows were wrinkled into a frown, and her eyes were even puffier than usual.

"Luana, qué pasó? You look awful," I said, grimacing at the sight of her bitten off skin.

"María, you didn't hear?" she whispered.

"Hear what?"

"Mariana. They fired her last night, pobrecita. She had already packed up and left before I could talk to her," she said. Immediately, chills formed on the back of my neck. My mind jumped to the thought of her taking her son, packing what few things they had, and moving again, only to find another sewing job that would only make enough to buy twenty-five cent ramen at the corner store. "And that poor kid," she continued, "she can't even pay for his daycare at this point."

"Luana, we gotta do something." I muttered. "This is the third one in the last month," I said, my voice raising with anger.

"Shh," she said, nudging my leg as the bus driver gave us a judging look in the rear view mirror. "Oye, María. You wanna get outta that place? Then you've got the best shot out of all of us. You've been in the States the longest. And you're the only one who can read English good," she said, turning back to look out the window.

"Yeah?" I whispered back. "And where has that got me?" I questioned impatiently.

"No sé, okay. Lo que sea, María," she said, rolling her eyes and standing as the bus came to a halt. I shook my head and piled off the bus with the others, though the conversation with Luana left an odd taste in my mouth.

The *click clack* of padlocks fastening shut marked the beginning of another grueling eleven hour day. The door had seemingly rusted over even more in the past day in mourning of Mariana. The steel beams that surrounded it were discolored so much to the point of being green. The floor to ceiling windows just past the door made it even worse; the sky, though grey, taunted me from behind the door. Even the murky clouds were calling my name, only to be locked away through the steel slab in front of me.

"Listen up, ladies," Mark called from the front of the room. "Inspection day is one day away. Clean up your scraps. Keep your workspaces neat. I don't wanna hear any complaining, or crying, or whining. And cover your cuts or scrapes. The last thing I need is someone filing complaints against us," he snarled.

Sighing, I swept scraps of fabric off my desk and headed over to the trash can to dispose of them. Inspection felt like more stress for me than the factory itself. The inspector would check everything from the paint on the walls to our workspaces, which Mark insisted we tidy obsessively. Dropping the scraps into the can below, I noticed a thick book laying on top of the trash. Picking it out gingerly, I held it up to see the front cover, which read *State of California Labor Laws and Violations*. I squinted to ensure I was really reading the title correctly. Blinking again, the title remained the same. I hustled back to my seat, keeping the treasure wrapped in the loose fabric of my sweater before slipping it into my bag. I pulled my sweater sleeve up slyly to peek at my watch. *Eight more hours?* My restless mind was already anxious for the end of the day. My hands trembled with adrenaline as I struggled to push the thread through the needle.

"María, you alright?" Luana asked.

"Yeah, yeah. I'm fine," I whispered, hearing Mark's footsteps behind me. "Just - talk to you later, okay?" I said, finally threading the needle.

Seven hours, fifty-six minutes, and thirty-three seconds to go.

Click click! The sound of the locks popping open was even more beloved than usual. I stuffed my pay into my jacket pocket and sprinted to the bus. As soon as my body hit the seat, my hands rushed to open my find.

"María, what's that?" Luana questioned as she sank down in the seat next to me. My eyes fluttered across the page as they read the words printed below.

"Code 329: Unpaid overtime. Code 266: Verbal abuse. Code 567: Hazardous working conditions," I muttered.

"María, what are you talking about?" she inquired.

"Look at this. Mira, aquí," I said, pointing to the words on the page. Her expression became frustrated as her eyes tried to make sense of the print. "They're the violations Mark always talks about in his inspection speeches," I said excitedly.

"Yeah? Where'd you find something like that?" she asked, raising her penciled eyebrows at me.

"En la basura. I don't think Mark thought any of us would be able to read it."

"Oh yeah? You gonna do something, chica?," she said, shrugging.

"Sí, I am. I'm just not sure what yet," I mumbled, leafing through the pages.

"Well you better figure it out fast. Inspection is twelve hours away, tú sabes," she responded matter-of-factly. As the bus screeched to a halt, I jumped up to run off, my mind still somersaulting in thought.

"Buenas noches, Luana," I called over my shoulder as I stumbled down the steep stairs.

The sound of rapidly flipping pages was now a constant hum in the room. My fingertips grew raw against the stiff paper. My eyes, still bloodshot, were glued to the small, black type. A seed of heat and anger spread through my chest as I read each line.

The long hours. The slaps across the face. The chemical air we breathed. The door that sealed us shut. Even the under the table pay, which Mark himself had assured us was only saving us tax money. They had been illegal the whole time.

"Mamá, you're home!" Luis's voice interrupted my thoughts as he stumbled out of the hallway, wrapping me in a hug.

"Yes, love," I said, cupping his soft face in my hands.

"Did you find out if I can go on the trip?" he asked, his eyes pleading for a positive response.

"Not yet, mijo. But I promise you, I will know very soon," I sighed. Rubbing his back to comfort him, a sharp pain shot through my hand as my hangnail caught on his shirt tag. Unhooking it, I read the small text covering the tag. My fingers ran over the embroidered words again, noticing the loose thread I had just pulled with my nail. *100% Cotton. Cold Wash. Made in the USA.*

"What's wrong, Mamá?" Luis asked as he pulled away. A smile was slowly spreading on my face as pieces connected in my mind.

8

"Nothing, mijo. Time to go to sleep," I said, shooing him away. The girls at the factory may have not been able to read; but, if there was one thing we could do, it was sew.

"Inspection day ladies! Less talking and more sewing!" Mark yelled. My machine fluttered rapidly as I shoved more fabric through it. The girls around me exchanged anxious glances as they sewed. Even Luana, with her usually confident presence, looked preoccupied as she threaded another needle. I tried to smile back to calm their nerves, but only found myself trembling with the same nervous energy.

"And here we have our production facility," I heard Mark say as he and the inspector entered through the back.

I could feel the uneven breaths of every girl around me halt as the inspector made his way around the room. Even through the hum of the machines, the sound of the inspector's dry hands flipping each page on his clipboard cut through the air like a freshly sharpened knife. As he approached Mariana's old station, I heard the clicking of his expensive shoes stop.

"Empty station?" he questioned, still keeping his eyes locked on the forms in front of him.

"Um, yes. But, just today," Mark interjected, wiping his palms on his dress pants. "Called in sick. Flu season, you know?" he chuckled unconvincingly. The inspector's eyebrows raised as he scribbled more on the page with his black pen and continued on his rounds, making an abrupt stop at my station.

"Last one?" he asked, his eyes finally leaving the page to look over at my table. I nodded, leaning back to reveal my workspace. My scraps had been thrown out, the table cleaned of its usual dust and grime. Its splintering wood had been disguised with a few swipes of sandpaper. I could feel the watchful eyes of the inspector as he observed my table for any signs of safety violations.

"Would you mind just moving that shirt so I can see the whole workspace?" he asked politely, gesturing towards the nearly finished blouse on the table. As slyly as I could manage with fluttering hands, I pushed back the shirt collar to reveal the obnoxiously large tag. On it I had sewn: *Code 329 . 266 . 567.*

Keeping my head low, I raised my eyes to watch the inspector's attention suddenly change focus. The furious black pen stopped its writing suddenly. The sound of flipping pages was interrupted by one final, furious scribble before the clicking of his expensive shoes grew faint again. My tense shoulders relaxed back into their typical slouch.

"You'll be hearing from us soon," he said bluntly, shaking Mark's sweating hand. His face bore no expression. I could see the hope of myself and every other woman in the room walking right past us as he headed towards the loathed door. As he pushed out, his hands graced over the rusted metal. His fingers traced the holes which the padlocks filled every day as his eyebrows furled in sudden understanding. The barely glowing light lit the smallest halo in his deep eyes. As I prepared to watch him slip away, my eyes locked with his firm gaze as he gave a slow nod and backed away through the steel doorway, which closed with its typical *thud.*

❧ ❧

"Mamá, good bye! I'll see you tonight!"

"Ay, mijo," I called. "Have a great day, my love. You deserve it," I said as I handed him a brown paper bag with his lunch.

"Thank you, Mamá," he said, leaving a kiss on my cheek.

"You have the envelope, mijo? Don't lose that," I warned, checking the front pocket of his backpack one more time to make sure the crisp fifty dollar bill was zipped away safely.

"Yes, Mamá," he smiled, wrapping me in another hug. A warm smile spread over my face as I watched him finally leave on his first field trip.

My watch revealed that the time was a peaceful 8:30. The television was on from last night, the telenovela still blaring. On the television stand was the newspaper that had just been delivered, lying face up. A white paper pinned onto the right hand corner concealed the headline.

To María - I know it's been a long few months, but the case closed today. I congratulate you and the other girls on your win. Take a look at the headline.

My hand reached to eagerly peel away the paper to reveal the large print. It read, *Los Angeles Sweatshop Closed: Hundreds of Women Reimbursed for Unpaid Labor.*

A Sunlit Cigarette

My family collectively set out on a secretive mission to reverse my persistent old school fashion. After countless attempts, they have yet to tear down my stubborn walls and persuade me into buying one of those gadgets that all the kids these days are glued to.

"Grandpa, it's time for you to evolve with the 21st century," my granddaughter lightheartedly expressed.

"I know an iPhone may be too complicated for you, but what if we got you an iPad for your birthday? We want you to join Facebook, you'd love it! You can even read the paper on there instead of trudging outside in the cold every morning," she pronounced with a definitive eagerness in her voice.

My daughter Camille approached me from behind, placing her hand on my shoulder, comforting the aches and pains which exhausted my elderly body.

"Dad, you won't have to worry about bending down and hurting your back when you pick up the paper anymore," Camille added.

"What am I to do with some fancy technology when my vision gets blurrier by the day? What I could really use is some new eyesight!" I smiled, and felt my face align with wrinkles.

I felt genuine sorrow for my grandchildren. They would never experience the ecstasy of putting pen to paper, or the satisfaction of thrusting a handwritten letter off into a mail slot. They would never feel the delight of walking outside in a robe and slippers to retrieve a freshly tossed newspaper in a sea of green grass coated by morning dew.

I vow to be the man who bends down and picks up the newspaper every single morning– even if it kills me.

❧ ❧

My daughter and granddaughter had stopped by for a visit accompanied by warm cups of flavored coffee, which filled my house with a pleasant aroma on that crisp Sunday morning. Ever since my wife's passing, my family would stop by every so often to chat in my decrepit yet charming house to assure themselves that I was doing just fine on my own. My children had this underlying fear that I had become a complete recluse and spent all of my time with my nose in a newspaper or book.

My granddaughter came over in hopes of gaining my personal insight on the Vietnam War for a school project- a war that I had written endless articles about. It was the war that I experienced secondhand through my many interviewees of American soldiers and their families during the 70's. Three cups of coffee and two hours later, I had told her everything my rusted brain could recall—from the gory details I exploited in articles, down to the day President Nixon called it quits.

Soon after they left, I decided to delve deeper into the past and ventured to the ominous basement that I hadn't walked down to in years. With barely any daylight shining through the window at the top right corner of the basement, I grabbed a flashlight and nervously flicked it on. With one hand on the splintering railing and the other trembling while holding a flashlight, I stepped onto the wooden staircase.

I took in a gulp of air, relieved that I had made it down safely. My lungs distressed from years of smoking cigarettes got a small reprieve as I took a moment to catch my breath. Glancing around, it was astounding to see the stacks of newspapers which flooded my basement. My eyes widened as I stood there stunned by the stacks upon stacks of the past which had quietly sat in my basement for years, tucked away from the rest of the world.

Dust covered the newspapers like a thick blanket and I had to wipe it off with my bare hand to be able to read the headlines. My journalistic passion had kicked in full gear, I was tingling with exuberance, and felt entirely in my element. It was like watching my life back as a movie while

I uncovered the dust from *The New York Times*, most of which bore front pages were written by myself. I traveled through decades studying the articles and reminisced on a life and career I poured my soul into.

In the midst of the shuffle of newspapers, a randomly placed black leather notebook appeared in between the 1973 issues of *The New York Times*. As I forced the notebook open, the stench of old, rusted paper pervaded my nose. I instantly noticed a hole burned through the first page about the size of a cigarette and a familiar black ink drawing of a sun. A pang of guilt suddenly shot through my stomach. A piece of my past that I had buried and forgotten about was suddenly revived and forcing its way back into my life. I knew exactly who this notebook belonged to.

Taken aback by this finding, I propped myself on the newspapers which were now tossed into one enormous pile, rather than neatly stacked the way they were found.

My curiosity and excitement had overwhelmed my hands, causing me to nearly tear the first page of the notebook in half as I flipped to the next one. To my amazement, an entry was scribbled in hard black ink on the second page. I was allured by what this journal had in store and astounded by the fact that a vital piece of my past was lodged in between those stacks for decades without my knowledge.

October 13, 1973

Feeling your hand gently grasp a thousand dollar painting, lifting it off the wall, and bolting out of a gallery is an inexplicable thrill. Just thinking about that last piece I stole, and I can immediately feel my body pulsing with adrenaline, nerves electrifying, and heart beating. I have explored the spontaneity of tattoos, felt the momentary euphoria from many drugs, and made memories that most people would shudder at, but nothing compares to art theft. I have never felt more alive, present, or valuable.

Gala Voleur was a mystery. Everyone became accustomed to both her name and her legacy, but no one knew inside her story.

Except for me.

I became engulfed in Gala's world. All her colors, elements, and designs. She let me in and I was consumed. Gala was a woman with a tough exterior, but inside lay an innocent and trapped child. The tattoos that painted her body were a facade, covering scars and hiding any sign of suffering or weakness from the world. Gala's petite body and emerald eyes contrasted with her edgy conveyance. She was a beautiful, yet deceptive, piece of art; an optical illusion of some sort.

There were myths told of Gala that, to many, would be deemed almost unbelievable. I had heard people exclaim that she sold her stolen paintings to become a multi-millionaire. A toothless, hunchbacked old woman who once stood beside me on a crowded subway, told a tale of Gala and her sixth sense for interacting with the dead, and how she'd met the soul of Vincent Van Gogh in a sunflower field.

I asked all around New York City about her- both when I was connected to her and when she became a mystical figure who vanished into thin air- I longed to know people's perceptions and the story they'd gathered. I seemed to be thirsting for any tidbit of information I could contrive about Gala, yet, I had once been accustomed with each and every layer of her soul that I myself unraveled. I'd felt her deepest wounds and I'd heard her darkest secrets.

As life moved forward, it seemed, my memory of her faded more and more.

1973 was the year I began my dream job as a journalist at *The New York Times*. I had my spot in the paper, but only if this first article of mine thrived. I was incredibly close to making it, as long as I came up with something intriguing and unique. My boss was a plump, bald man who held a short temper and talked with as much energy and vigor as a sales auctionist. I vividly recall him yelling in my young, fresh out-of-college face.

"If you think you can make it here with your first article being about the war, the goddamn Beatles and their goddamn hippy folks, or something to do with the Brady Brunch you're cut–got that son?" He made no exceptions and had no remorse. He cut right to the chase and I appreciated that.

"Yes, sir," I looked to my potential new boss and assertively responded. I felt as if I were sixteen again, answering to my strict father. This gave me a sense of familiarity in a foreign setting.

I was sweating profusely, overwhelmed and dazed by the chaos that surrounded me. There were telephones buzzing left and right and a fury of men and women running around like frantic squirrels in search of the last acorn. I was in the arena, ready to fight.

It was an unstable, yet exhilarating, period of my life. In short terms, no story meant no job. I was reporting, interviewing, and type writing at all hours of the day. My unkempt shoe box Brooklyn apartment was covered in newspapers, records, and books, yet empty and missing that warm home embrace. I was fascinated by news and awake by drinking ungodly amounts of cheap coffee. My life rotated on this schedule for what felt like an eternity. Work, home, and then more work at home. I had two weeks for my make-it or break-it article to be rejected and torn apart or published in *The Times*. I scrapped several storylines within that time frame, constantly thought about ideas, gathered information, and then struggled to execute a successful story up to my boss' and my own standards. I was suddenly working against the clock and not with it. Time had turned on me and I found myself frustrated and fresh out of ideas.

And then came Gala.

I cocked my head back against a stack of newspapers as I felt blood coursing through my veins. My memory of her came firing back, and my mind had erupted in flames.

October 14, 1973

Today began the way each day does. I was awakened to the sound of Bob Dylan faintly playing in the background while discovering my body twisted on a broken sofa in an unknown borough of New York. I walked around all morning and shoved a bagel down my bell bottoms just in case hunger struck. Before afternoon hit, I had gone through half a pack of smokes. My gut felt uneasy and having a cigarette in my mouth provided me with a sense of security in this lonely, chaotic city. My mind wandered aimlessly as I motioned through the streets of New York. I observed the faces that piled on the streets of businessmen in suits, young children grasping their mother's hand, and office employers trolling on by. I decided to write and sit beneath one of the only trees in Manhattan, which appears to be the sole source of oxygen in this factory and cigarette smoke polluted city. As I'm sitting here, cigarette in mouth and pen in hand, I wonder what my next piece will be-maybe a Picasso, a Monet, perhaps? I wonder when I'll be able to hold someone's masterpiece in my arms again, against my own flesh. Holding on to something valuable again something that will become mine.

The paper of the journal crinkled as I held it between my thumb and forefinger. The page was rough from years of lying in a darkened basement, untouched, and seemingly rotting away between a stack of ancient newspapers. My memory of Gala and the struggles I encountered as an aspiring journalist remained forgotten for decades, that is, until now.

I vividly recall how I wasn't looking for anybody— I was focused on my article, declaring a permanent spot in *The New York Times*, and my rapidly approaching deadline. She looked in need. Hell, everyone in the city looked in need of a hug, a friend, or a cigarette. But she needed something in that moment and so did I. She caught my eye sitting under that single, misplaced tree in Manhattan, forcing my feet stopped right in their tracks.

"Can I bum a smoke?" I found myself confused and surprised by this impulsive action. They say to not judge a book by its cover, but one glance at her made me want to read the whole damn novel.

"Sure, why the hell not."

The angelic and soft voice that poured out of this woman shocked me, for her appearance made her seem bizarre and edgy. My eyes instantly wandered off to the simple black outline of the sun which was delicately placed on the left side of her neck. There wasn't a cloud in the sky, yet the wind rustled the orange leaves on the tree which canopied her. I placed my briefcase down, wiggled my tie, and ran my hand through my thick flowy brown hair. It felt right to sit beneath the only tree in New York City on that fall afternoon and share a cigarette or two with a mysterious woman.

A pack of cigarettes later, and I became entranced by Gala Voleur. Day crept into night as we sat beneath that tree. I could have sat there talking to her through all the seasons. I could've watched those orange leaves fall off by her side, beared a snowstorm, and then watch as the leaves blossomed again in the spring with her. While I am unable to recall what we endlessly chattered about, I can vividly picture how a few strands of her brunette hair brushed against her cheek, how her large green eyes gleamed, and how reserved yet open she was. The concept of time did not bombard my mind that afternoon, nor did the unwritten article which typically lingered in each and every one of my thoughts.

Gala was intriguing and unique. What I was so desperately in search of for an article, I had found in a person.

October 23, 1973

No one had ever wanted to play hopscotch with me in kindergarten or had the desire to hold my hand and take me out to a dance. It's different with Wyatt; he's interest in my thoughts, my favorite records, and even what my tattoos symbolize. He values me as if I were a magnificent piece of art. I told him all about my secret practice— how I've managed to establish a fulfilling career through a felonious act. Interestingly enough, I felt Wyatt's fondness of me grow from this wild revelation. He was not only intrigued, but entirely engaged in my thoughts and stories. Last night he told me that if he saw me in a museum, he'd steal me right off the wall. Everything about him screams normalcy: his ties, work hours, and polite manners. But for some unknown reason, I am completely and utterly drawn to him- he makes me feel like I have meaning in this world. Wyatt observes me the way art admirers observe a painting, appreciating

19

my colors, my textures, and understanding my purpose. No one has ever observed or valued me as such.

It was lust. I knew it then and I know it now. What Gala and I shared was a passionate entanglement, but it was not love. We spent most nights of our two short weeks together laying in my bed. She'd rest her head against my leg while we stared at the dirty ceiling of my apartment and shared a pack of smokes and a story.

Gala became the subject for my first article— the article that determined my life's fate. She was an intriguing storyline that I had fallen in love with. I gathered quotes and information from her while holding her hand, or gently tugging strands of her soft brunette hair behind her ear, or even while we would lay in bed sharing a cigarette together. Without her knowledge, she was being interviewed for *The New York Times* as she shared her life and revealed the method behind her madness; why she stole art.

Gala had been neglected her entire life until I came along. She described being thrown into the world with absolutely no direction or hand to hold. She was a free, roaming soul in the city. The value people find in paintings is what Gala had longed for people to find in her. She grew obsessed with stealing valuables, hoping for someone to value her the way people value and perceive a piece like the Mona Lisa.

My article on the New York City Art Thief ended up roaring with success. My boss ate the story up and was in absolute awe that I got a criminal to cooperate and sit down for an interview with me. But I didn't view Gala as a criminal- to me, she was a lost, lonesome woman in dire need of love and affection.

At the time, I hadn't considered what would happen between Gala and me after that article was published. The possibility of her getting arrested or locked away in prison hadn't crossed my mind. The desire to be successful overpowered my inner conscience, which to this day weighs heavy for having exploited someone who was already so alone and damaged.

The last memory I shared with Gala was on a cloudless October day. I carefully placed my right hand on the sun tattooed on her neck while she snagged the cigarette out of my mouth and took a drag. While looking into her emerald eyes, I slowly dragged my fingertips across the permanently engraved sun on her skin, before I turned and walked down the stairs to the subway that would transport me to *The New York Times* where I'd submit the article that would either land me a career, or leave me wholly discouraged and broken.

October 30, 1973

Wyatt, I trusted you. I regret falling into your trap and being a naive woman who believed that your interest in me was genuine, and without selfish intentions. Now I know that when you looked into my eyes that I wasn't the light in your life; I was simply a subject to manipulate and use to your advantage. It was all a lie. You were a fake, deceptive, bullshit lie. You ignited the light in me, and now all I see is darkness. I hope when you discover this you are engulfed with guilt and find it impossible to appreciate the sun's warmth without my face haunting all of your happy, cloudless days. I now know my worth, and how it truly is nothing. I will never be valuable.

- Gala Voleur

I closed the notebook and felt my heart violently thumping and eyes staring off into space. In the dimness of the basement, I looked down at the journal laying in my hand— the same hand that had once felt the sun on Gala's skin. The journal, which sat in my clammy palm, was suddenly illuminated by a single source of light, similar to the way a spotlight focuses in on a performer on stage. I looked up to the window in the corner of the basement and noticed that it was a gloomy, dark day, making this occurrence an inexplicable oddity. There were no words that could explain the spectacle before my eyes. I felt Gala's presence shine through as I held the journal in my hand and tightly pressed it against my throbbing chest.

The basement door then plunged open, causing my body to shudder.

"Dad, are you alright?" my daughter cried out while launching herself down the uneven stairs.

"Camille, I am fine," I said reassuringly.

She then knelt by my side with a look of bewilderment expressed on her face and a bead of sweat aligned at the top of her forehead. I felt her heavy breath brush against my cheek as she latched her hand onto my shoulder.

"I can see clearly now," I mumbled under my breath.

Agrostophobia

My father claims his experiences in Vietnam led to his Agrostophobia; the fear of grass. Everytime he would see even a blade of grass, his fight or flight mechanism triggered. Unable to move because of his temporary paralysis, he would fall to the floor convulsing violently. Hell, he couldn't even look out the window because if he saw the lawn, he would be shell-shocked. I can recall on one occasion delivering the Valedictory speech at my high school graduation. As my eyes scanned the crowd to find my family, I was able to see my mother, sitting in her seat, eyes wide, beaming with pride. But to her right sat a hole-an empty chair amongst the sea of family members there to celebrate their children's achievements. That hole became symbolic for our family's relationship with the man that was supposed to be there, my father. When I asked her where he'd been-why he hadn't made it, her eyes wouldn't even meet mine, they'd just fall straight to the floor.

"He's home… I couldn't get him out of the house tonight."

That was the first time I'd seen his fear take control of him-the first time that it began to impact our family.

Once, I remember being woken out of a dead sleep at 3:00 a.m. to my father's screams. Upon rushing to his room, I found my mother rubbing his back.

"He just had a bad dream, sweetie, go back to bed," she said to me. My vision was hazy from the sleep that I'd just woken up from, but I could clearly see the look on my mother's face. We both knew that something was deeply rooted within my father, and there was no doubt that he was suffering from a bad dream for sure, but this fear of his, is one that he won't be able to easily wake up from.

"Mom, you know I have work tomorrow morning, I can't just wake up in the middle of the night, every single night like this," I said back to her while rubbing my eyes. "This is really tiring," I remember thinking to myself as I began to drift back to sleep.

There was one day where we had picked him up from treatment, only for him to return to being the Father I had known before the fear took hold of him and he became the scared man who had been scarred from the war. This was the case on many days. My dad would be fine after we'd pick him up from treatment, only to find that ten hours later, the fear would take hold of him again. On one occasion, my father refused to get out from under his covers due to the grip that the fear had on him. It seemed that the only thing that could bring him any sort of comfort was his bed-it was his safety net; his area of refuge. After many instances of this, it began to weigh so heavily on us that we started losing hope-it seemed nothing would work.

I was at the grocery store with my father when I happened to glance at the community bulletin board that hung at the front of the store. The words *Specialized therapy for veterans of the Vietnam War suffering from PTSD* stuck out like a sore thumb on the stark white flier that hung from the board. After countless failed attempts at getting my father the help he needed, we'd all but given up that there was anything actually out there that could do something to help my father get his life back. Ripping the flier from the board, I folded it up and shoved it in my pocket-at this point, we were pulling at straws-we were willing to try anything.

Pulling into the driveway, my father opened the door, careful that we were parked directly in the middle of the pavement-nowhere near the grass-and quickly walked towards the front door with me. Walking in the house, my mother greeted us, smiling back.

"How was work?" She asked, as she watched me walk past her. Before I could reply, she said, "What's this?" picking up the flier that I put on the table. She eyes skimmed the lines of the paper until they fell on the part that read, *Specialized therapy for veterans of the Vietnam*

War suffering from PTSD. She looked back at me with a questioning look. "What's this supposed to be?"

"It's therapy," I responded, "for dad."

"You know that your father doesn't respond well to therapy, what makes you think this one will be any different? Everytime we bring him to therapy, he either doesn't get along with the therapist, or we see short-term changes for a few hours, only to have him then grow more afraid later that very same day." my mother exclaimed, it was obvious that she'd become hopeless of the idea that my father would ever lead a normal life again, one free of panic every time he sees the front lawn.

"He can at least give it a try... there's a meeting for the group this Friday. There's no harm in that, is there? I just want to see him get better. We're out of options here and nothing that we've tried in the past has worked." I begged my mother.

I'd too, grown hopeless-- watching my mother believe that nothing would work instilled a fear inside of me. Anxiety was flooding my brain, all I could think about was a normal, happy life for my father, and for myself. For once, I decided to take matters into my own hands, hoping that my father would see the concern in my eyes and my desire for him to get better would spark a desire in him too.

Later into the night, I approached my father to ask him about the subject. My palms grew sweaty as I approached him. Growing the courage, I tried to find the words that might bring my father to see past his fear and finally see reason.

"Hey dad, can I talk to you for a minute?" Not even glancing in my direction, he remained in place, fixed on the tv. "Dad?"

"What do you want," he shot back.

Carefully pulling out the folded-up flier from my pocket, I said to him, "Well, there's this group that meets on Fridays... they are all Vietnam veterans... I was just won-"

"No," he interrupted as he abruptly turned to face me.

"Dad, at least give it a shot, you didn't even let me finish what I was gonna say."

"Why should I? None of the other groups have ever worked, they are all just a load of crap," he said, as his face grew bright red.

My face bore a look of desperation, "Dad, please."

"No, and that's that. Now go away."

And without another word, I walked away, defeated look filling my entire face.

I sulked back into the kitchen, where my mom was still sitting quietly doing her work on her laptop, just like she did everyday when she got home. She sat hunched over in the chair, exhausted from days of dealing with her husband's agonizing fear. Her face looked worn out, tired and hopeless. I stood there debating whether my hopeful outlook was worthy of vocalizing to my defeated mother. I couldn't fathom what had made me want to bring the flier home. What had I thought would have happened-a miraculous change somehow? Would he suddenly have been open to something he had sworn off for years? What was I thinking?

"So, did you ask dad about the counseling?" My mother asked.

"Yes," I hesitantly replied while nervously rubbing the top of as my eyes stared down at the kitchen floor.

"And what did he say?" she further questioned, as she turned around to face me.

"Well, he wasn't completely into the idea, he said no." As I spoke those words, I grew even more hopeless.

"I knew it, your father is quite stubborn," my mother exclaimed.

"Damn right he is, so what should we do about it? We have to get him to this therapy, his current state is ruining not only his life, but ours too," I pronounced, throwing the truth out there. It was time for my mother and I to fully acknowledge the depth of his fear.

Suddenly, it hit me, this trick would be cliche as all hell, but I figured we could try it. "Mom, what if we took him out to 'eat', but instead of eating, we would be secretly bringing him to the counseling. Maybe if he saw the actual group, he would be more inclined to attend their sessions."

My mother paused in her place, lifting her fingers from the keyboard, momentarily pausing from the furious typing she'd been engaged in. Looking up, her eyes met mine in a gaze as I nervously awaited her answer.

"That idea doesn't sound like it's going to work, but I guess it's all we have left to try."

Relieved that my mom hadn't belittled me because of my outlandish proposal,

"Thanks mom, do you want to tell dad about our 'dinner' plan, or should I?" I asked, half suppressing a devious smile.

I came home on Thursday evening to see my father lying face-down on the couch with my mother by his side. I immediately rushed over to him,

"Dad, are you okay?" I asked as I cast a look of concern on my face.

"He's fine," replied my mother as she rubbed his back,

"He saw a blade of grass on my shoe when I came home from work." my mother expressed. My mind went blank, I wasn't even a bit phased by this news.

I layed in bed that night, allowing my thoughts to consume my mind and deprive me of sleep. The sight of green grass and my father's terrified face ruminated in my mind, like a broken record, the image just kept replaying.

The next morning, my mother, father and I got into the car.

"This isn't a restaurant," said my father in an angry tone, as our car pulled into the building with the therapist's office. He cast his unforgiving gaze to me. "Son, where are we?"

"Dad, we are at the therapist's office."

"What did I tell you abo-"

"Dad. "You need the treatment. Please go, for us?"

I could see the angriness building in his eyes.

"No, I said no and that is final," my father said as he remained firmly planted in the car. Out of nowhere, my mom approached the car and grabbed my father by the arm. As she began dragging my father by the arm, my father cried out "What are you doing woman?" As we entered the therapist's office we were greeted by a charming, "Why hello there, you must be the Stevens family!" Standing in front of us was a man, no older than 30 years of age, dressed sharply in a business suit. His blonde locks were swept towards the right side of his head, and his blue eyes pierced my soul. "My name is Dr. Patterson, but you can just call me Pat. It's nice to see you made it out here tonight!" Unable to comprehend just how charismatic this man before me was, I said, "Uh, you're the therapist for the Vietnam Veterans, right?" "Yup that's me!" he replied.

At first, I couldn't tell if the smile that he had been wearing since we got here was a smile of conceit or of genuine happiness. How could this be the therapist for the Vietnam Vets? I pictured him as being some old guy who could barely walk, yet he was this sharply-dressed young man who couldn't be much older than me. He walked towards my father, "Nice to meet you! You must be Frank right?" My father quietly grumbled back to him, "Yes, that's me." "It's a pleasure to meet you Mr. Stevens, hopefully I can help you with the problems you've been going through!" "Good luck,"replied my father bluntly. Pat and the group of veterans, my father included, all went around the room, explaining their problems to each other. At the start, my father didn't talk at all, but as the meeting went on my father seemed to feel more welcomed by the group, to the point where he actually started talking. This was something new to my mother and I. Out of the countless therapy sessions my father had attended, he had barely even spoken. Now, upon being introduced to this new therapist, he's able to speak to him as comfortably as he would to one of his long time friends. I couldn't tell what it was about Pat that made him so likeable. Was it his charismatic personality? Was it his charming looks? I didn't really care, so long as my father was getting the help that he so desperately needed.

"Thank you for joining us today, Mr. Stevens! Hope you can join us next week!" called Pat as my father, my mother and I were walking towards the door. Upon hearing this, my father stopped dead in his tracks, and I saw him do something that I had never seen him do since I was a child. He smiled. "Thank you, Pat." said my father as he walked out of the door. As I looked back before closing the car door, I could see Pat smiling back at us. As we got back into the car, my mother asked my father, "So, what did you think of Dr. Patterson's therapy?" My father sat there for a few minutes, as if he was thinking of the perfect response to my mother's simple question. After what seemed like hours of wait-ing, he turned to my mother and simply responded, "Hey, that's pretty good." I could see the happiness on my mother's face as she heard this answer. This would be the first step to getting our father to be able to come back to our lives.

The very next week, my mother, my father, and I all returned to Dr. Patterson's office. Upon opening the door, we were greeted by Pat's unmistakeable charismatic voice.

"Welcome back Stevens family!" he said as he shook my father's hand.

"Glad to see you decided to attend another session," Dr. Patterson exclaimed with a beaming smile across his face. He motioned for my father to come into the room with the rest of the group while my mother and I sat patiently in for his session to be over.

As my mother and I sat side by side, I watched her nervously twiddled her thumbs and heard her sighing and taking in deep breaths. As I sat there with a blank expression of my face, but a mind filled with thoughts, my mother had broken the silence between us.

"These past few weeks, your father has been quite different. A good kind of different-- a slow but steady improvement even," my mother exclaimed as I turned my gaze towards her.

"What do you mean mom?" I asked, excited to hear some more hopeful thoughts from her.

"He's been much less grumpy, and for the first time in ages, he actually started a conversation with me," said my mom,

"It's like he's a whole new man." She broadly exclaimed.

I gently peeled the curtain back to look into the room where the therapy session was being held. Among the large circle of other war heroes, I spotted my dad. With a smile across his face, and a certain aura that ignited pure joy within me. This was sight I've been yearning to see, a face clear all terror and fear.

"So how long do you think he will need the therapy, mom?"

"I'm not sure... but we will be here to support him, no matter how tough the going gets."

"I can agree with that," I said while flashing a smile.

Weeks went by and my father's fear of grass slowly diminished. His fear had not controlled each and every thought or action he pursued. No longer was he the grouchy old veteran who spent his remaining golden years wasting away, silently watching tv on the couch. Instead, he was now a more sociable person. He even ate with the family now, talked to us, and managed to look out the window and peer at the lawn.

That Friday, we went to Dr. Patterson's therapy session. We entered to see the same, old cheery-faced, Pat as he welcomed back my father, along with the rest of us. "It's become almost like a routine now, you coming to the group I mean, Mr. Stevens," said Dr. Patterson. My mother and I sat down in the waiting room, just like the last several times.

Suddenly, Dr. Patterson, along with my father, flung the curtain separating the waiting room and the actual group therapy room wide open. He walked over to the front door as my father followed closely behind. Curious as to what was occurring outside, my mother and I walked over to the gaping doorway. Our jaws dropped with horror, as we spotted my father trembling on the front steps of the therapy office.

'Pat what are you doing?', I thought to myself, 'You are gonna mess up all of dad's progress!' I grew furious inside. I was quick to blame him-- my father had come so far, to have him go backwards was something unable to bear.

"Don't worry, I've got everything under control," said Pat as he backed further from the front steps of the therapy office and onto the grassy lawn. "Mr. Stevens, you'll never be able to overcome your fear unless you are able to face it," Dr. Patterson explained. He fixed his gaze back to my father,

"Now Frank, do it just like we practiced," he said in an uplifting voice.

"I... I don't know if I can Pat, I don't know if I'm ready..."

"Frank, think about your wife, your child... do you really want to appear like this in front of them? C'mon... show me the man that you showed me when we were practicing this on our own."

Trembling, I watched as my father's right foot slowly walked down the next step. He was shaking, visibly nervous. Suspense was in the air as the floorboards of the therapy office stairs creaked upon each of my father's steps. Now he was on the final step of the staircase.

If he took another shaking step, he would be face to face with daunting green grass, a fear that had consumed his life. The fear that ate away at his will to live. He knew he had already missed the potential to be the good father that he could have been while his son was growing up. Taking a deep breath, he lifted his foot off of the final step and firmly planted it onto the soft, wet grass below. I looked as my mother bursted into tears, overwhelmed with relief. As tears began to stream down her face, she knew the constant torment of my father's fear was over. The sight of my father stepping foot on green grass was undeniably amazing. I was in disbelief, surprised and delighted. I ran over to my father and gave him an open armed embrace. He stood there shocked and overwhelmed himself. It was a tiny step onto grass, but the biggest step my father would ever take.

Pat stood there grinning, proud and honored to help my father conquer his life altering fear.

"I'm so proud of you," My mother chimed in.

"Honey you overcame your fear, you really did," My mother managed to squeeze those words out between sobs.

My father, also tearing up, simply could not respond. He looked back at the two of us and said, "I think it's time to go back home, this is the start of a new life... a new beginning... I'm a new man now, the demons holding me back are gone now." And with that, we walked back to the car. My dad had become a new man, and it was all thanks to Dr. Patterson. Before I entered the car, I took one final glance at the therapy office. There it stood, still as antique as ever. I glanced down at the grass, now hopeful instead of resentful, for my father had overcome his fear

Day of Remembrance

Standing in front of the mirror and seeing myself in the same tuxedo I wore on my wedding day brought back many memories. Between the hundreds of guests downstairs, to the hours it'd taken the florist to set up the flower arrangements, transforming the church into what looked like a garden, today was supposed to be a day of happiness. However, this happiness was tempered by the overwhelming feeling of sadness-something that my daughter and I simply could not shake.

I just felt empty, like something was not there and needed to be. I glanced over to the mirror yet again and saw my beat-red face from the moments before I'd spent crying. I had always been a tough guy, not very emotional, but today I couldn't hold any of it back. Searching around the room for a tissue box, I made my way to the bathroom where one was sitting on the granite counter top. Wiping my eyes, I began to feel a sense of relief and the redness in my face was slowly fading away. I knew this day was going to painful to get through but I had no idea it was going to be this bad- this feeling of emptiness just would not go away long enough for me to feel any sort of happiness. I plopped myself down on the edge of the bed and took a deep breath, trying to relax.

Sitting on the bed looking out the window for quite some time now, I turned to the clock which read 4:25; I was expected to be down in my daughter's hotel room for 4:30, to escort her down to the ceremony, but I didn't know how I was going to pull myself together. I couldn't help but think of how my daughter was feeling today. This morning I woke up to a text from Elena saying, *I miss her dad*, and it brought tears to my eyes, which haven't stopped since. All a little girl dreams about is her wedding day being the happiest day of her life and now here we are, being overwhelmed with sadness- that was not expected six months ago. Flashbacks were constantly playing through my head, making it even harder to better my mood.

👁 👁

Standing on top of the rocks, I saw everything that lay before us-mountains and trees as far as I could see. Breathing heavy, I bent over, putting my hands to my knees, hoping to provide some relief to my lungs. And yet, even as I fought to control my breathing, with sweat running down my forehead, she looked more beautiful than ever. The five hour hike, coupled with my nerves getting the best of me, made my heart beat harder than it had in awhile. I had waited a long time for this moment-played it over and over again in my head but, it was better than I could have even imagined. Looking again at the mountains in front of me and taking as much of it in as I could, it hit me that this was the right thing to do. This would make me happy and with that, my heartbeat slowly began to relax.

"Remember our first hike up this mountain? You tripped over a rock and got a huge gash in your leg," I said looking up into her big blue eyes, while she tried to catch her breath.

"Yes," she said laughing, "and you wrapped your t-shirt around it to stop the bleeding."

Locking hands and sharing a quick smile, we walked over to a nearby bench we somehow always found ourselves at when we hiked this mountain that had a great view of the underlying mountains. While we sat on that bench overlooking the mountains, we reminisced some of our funny memories we shared together.

"And when we went to the Rolling Stones concert and you didn't want to pay for parking so we parked in some random parking lot and came out of the concert and the car was gone," Jane added.

"Yeah and we had to make an embarrassing phone call to your dad to come pick us up- man I thought he was going to kill me," we both couldn't stop laughing.

"Okay.. okay.. stop.. stop.. My stomach hurts-- from laughing-- so much," Jane tried to tell me but had a hard time getting it out because she was still laughing so hard. We laughed so hard, we were only able to get out a few words amidst the laughs.

Finally we were able to calm ourselves down, still giggling just a little. I turned to look at Jane as she was turned towards the view in front of her, staring until she turned her head to me and smiled subtly.

"Let's go check out that cliff over there," I suggested as we both stood up.

She gripped my hand tight and pulled herself closer to my body. Walking hand in hand, we made our way to the nearby cliff that overlooked the mountains. Placing my hand around her shoulders and giving her a tight squeeze I felt her golden brown hair brush over my arm while she turned her head as we shared a brief smile. The speed of my heart picked up the pace yet again, as she turned away, I closed my eyes for a quick second and took one, big, deep breath trying to slow down my breathing for my own good. These were going to be a few of the most important words to come out of my mouth and I'd be extremely embarrassed if I were to stutter and speak with a shaky voice.

I took another deep breathe just to be safe and held it in a little longer. My eyes remained closed but as I slowly opened them, I saw Jane still peering out at the mountains. Grabbing both of her hands, I looked into her eyes, and spoke a few simple words,

"Jane, it's been a crazy few years with you. Through the missing cars, adventurous summer nights, and the all the sweaty hikes, I've fallen deeper and deeper in love with you," I began what I thought was going to be a short speech. She smiled at me the whole time as words began to fly from my mouth and slowly, I could see her eyes begin to fill. "There hasn't been a single day that I have doubted what we have or shied away from the fact that I love you and wish to tell you that every waking moment of my life," I went on.

Despite my surprising calmness, I could feel my heart begin to beat fast again, my hands became shaky and clammy, but luckily my voice did not appear to be shaky-at least not to me. I lunged my foot out just a little ways and placed one knee the rocky dirt. The rocks may have even punctured my skin as my leg sat on top of them for a few seconds.

37

Jane's hands quickly found themselves covering her mouth and the tears that once only filled her eyes were now streaming down her face.

Without any hesitation I looked up at her and asked,

"Jane, will you marry me?"

"Oh my goodness, yes -of course-yes," she responded with a look of pure elation across her face. As my shaky hands placed the ring, I spent saving up for the past two years, on her finger, I was finally able to breathe. I quickly stood up before any words were shared and lifted her off her feet and swung her around in pure joy.

Glancing at the clock once again to see that it was 4:28, I realized I better head down to Elena's room. Buttoning my jacket, I quickly tied my shoes and picked the few pieces of lint from off my pants. Taking one last moment to look at myself in the mirror, I fixed the blue rose that sat on my lapel, thinking to myself that, if nothing else, I needed to keep it together for her. Today was about her. Breathing in deeply, I turned to the door and began walking to my daughter's room.

Walking down the hall, I began to picture Elena in Jane's wedding dress. The strapless gown fit Jane perfectly and looked just as beautiful on Elena. The detailing of the lace made them both look like angels. With each step, I began to feel the excitement that was supposed to be shared on the day of a wedding, but that was all brought to a sudden stop.

Behind the door I noticed Elena sitting in a room full of silence, head in hands, sobbing uncontrollably. She lifted her head up slowly from her hands and looked at me with bloodshot eyes. My heart dropped into my stomach and an overwhelming feeling of pure sorrow came upon me. As I walked farther into the room, the feeling intensified.

"Elena, what's the matter?" I asked, knowing very well the answer to my question. She immediately broke down and began sobbing even harder than before. I asked again, "Honey, tell me what's wrong," I said again after receiving no response. Still she couldn't seem to get words out of her mouth in between taking heavy breaths. Doing the only thing I knew to do in this situation, I wrapped my arms around her and pulled her in close hoping she would find some form of comfort.

"How can I just do this without her; it's so selfish of me," she said lifting her face from my shoulder and looking up to me. Taking her hand and looking into her eyes again, I could tell that she knew what I was going to say- the same thing I had been telling her through this whole process.

"You know that she would want this day to be perfect-like you guys talked about-even though she isn't here to share the time with you." I have told Elena this hundreds of times in different ways but I wanted her to get the point I was trying to make regardless how hard it is to accept.

"It just isn't fair, she should be here today sharing these moments with us. It has been months already and it still hasn't gotten any easier," she began crying out with a beat red face. Her breath was heavy as she continued to sob. "I just constantly wonder why, why did this have to happen?" she broke down as her head fell onto my shoulder.

I was at a loss for words, and didn't have an answer to why, no one did. Months have passed and still every morning, we both wake up wondering when the pain will stop, when we will stop feeling sorry for ourselves, but quite frankly, I don't think it ever will. We will always wake up wishing she were here and that's what everyone does when they lose a loved one. But I know for a fact, and I am sure Elena knows as well, that Jane would want us to keep living our lives even if she cannot be here.

Elena continued, "I thought I would be okay today, a little sad yeah, but I didn't think it would be this overwhelming. I don't know how to do this dad, I really don't know."

I felt helpless, like there was nothing say to Elena will help her feel any better, because I myself, was not feeling any ounce of happiness right now.

"I know honey, I know, but she would want us to continue living and you know that," I said as I attempted to wipe her face with my thumb.

"Let's get you cleaned up and we will head down stairs, we wouldn't want anyone seeing you like this now would we?" I said hoping for a little bit of a chuckle.

Standing up, Elena wiped away her tears, which had now mixed with her eyeliner, creating long black streaks that ran across her cheeks and fingers. As she began towards the bathroom, my own breathing grew heavy as my lip began to quiver. Knowing that if Elena saw me break down, we'd be back to square one, I bit down on my lip and quickly walked to the bathroom. Pulling open the handle, I walked in and slid up against the inside of the door, bolting the lock behind me as my own tears began to find their way from my eyes.

Sliding lower and lower, my feet began to come out from under me and I quickly found myself on the cold cement floor of the bathroom, unable to move. In the midst of trying to catch my breath I heard a faint knock on the door. I froze due to the thought that it could be Elena knocking and knowing that she couldn't see me like this.

"One second," I said from the bathroom floor. Springing up onto my feet, I took a look in the mirror to see the redness in my face and eyes that looked as if they had just been punched. I turned the faucet on and ran my fingers underneath it hoping it would warm up a bit. But time was ticking and more than a few seconds had passed, so I splashed the shockingly cold water on my face and reached for the face cloth that should be hanging up but wasn't. Reaching around the sink, eyes closed and water dripping down my face, I grabbed the towel and patted my face dry. Taking one last look in the mirror I felt relieved that my face was somewhat less red, still pretty red and puffy, but much better than before. Again, I heard a second knock on the door.

"Dad you in there?" a sweet innocent voice said through the still bolted bathroom door. Immediately I unbolted the door and cracked it open slowly, only hoping she wouldn't notice I had just been crying.

"Yes honey-sorry-I'm finished now, are you ready to --" I said looking up from the ground but only to stop mid sentence in awe. Tears, gone. Red eyes, gone. You could have never even guessed that she just spent the last 45 minutes or so sobbing.

She just smiled.

"Yes dad-I am ready-let's go down," she said reaching her hand out to grab my arm. We headed out the door and down to the ceremony.

Upon the opening of the big church doors, Jane's contagious laugh echoed through the room. Looking up, I was mesmerized by the dress I was not able to see until this moment. She told me about the "sweetheart neckline and the beautifully detailed lace bodice," if those are even the correct terms to be used. Without even thinking about it, my eyes began to fill just a bit with tears and a few fell onto my face. Wiping them off with my fingers, I looked down the aisle again to see Jane, still in shock over how gorgeous she looked. She turned to her father as they locked arms and took the first steps down the aisle with smiles on both of their faces. The long train of the gown followed behind her as she made her way towards me.

Then in the split of a second she was within an arm's reach of me. After sharing a hug and kiss with her father, I reached out to grab her hand. She clenched it tightly and stepped up onto the altar, with both of my hands interlocked with hers. Looking into those big blue eyes I mouthed,

"I love you."

She responded, "I love you too," and softly smiled as the justice of the peace began the ceremony.

She looked beautiful. The white lace gown her mother once wore looked stunning on my little girl. It fit her like a glove. Her and her mother were so similar it was almost as if I was looking at my wife standing in front of me. They shared the same big blue eyes that anyone could look into for hours. I couldn't believe the time had come for my daughter to walk down the aisle. It felt like just yesterday she was greeting me at the door with hugs and kisses when I came home from work. "Time really does fly," I thought to myself, looking at her for a second time.

"Elena, you look so beautiful," I said. I thought about saying something how my wife would be so proud of who she has become but I decided it would be a better idea to not mention it. Risking the tears that might accompany that comment wasn't worth it right now.

"Thanks Dad, Are you ready to do this?" She said to me as she attempted to fix the long lace train with the help of her bridesmaids. I turned to her and said, "The real question is, are you ready?"

"Yes I'm ready," She said grabbing my hand as we started making our way to the elevator to go downstairs for the ceremony. I could tell that something wasn't sitting well with her.

We got down to the big doors where hundreds of people sat waiting to hear the sound of the famous tune, "Here Comes the Bride." She stopped and grabbed my arm. That look of innocence crossed her face again, her eyes began to fill up and I thought to myself, "Oh no, not again." I didn't say a word, I just wrapped my arms around her again and she began to cry harder than before. I held her tight against my chest before she said anything.

"Dad I really don't think I can do this without her," she cried. Without saying anything, much of the reason being I didn't know what else to say, I just squeezed her tighter.

"It's just not fair, why did this have to happen, she should be here today and she's not," she said with even more tears rolling down her face as her freshly done makeup was seeping off.

"Come with me," I said to Elena.

"What," she responded as she followed me and we walked out the doors of the hotel into the fresh May air.

We walked up and down the sidewalks looking at all the flowers that were blooming for the spring time. There were too many flowers to count all of different colors, shapes and sizes. But one specifically stood out. Elena stopped when she saw it, picked one out of the ground and said, "These were her favorite, every few weeks or so she placed a vase full of them in the center of the dining room table, she always told me she thought they completed the room," she chuckled. I smiled at her and the purple mums she held in her hand. I could tell she was beginning to calm down, which was a big relief. We took a seat on a bench overlooking the garden but didn't say a word for some time until I broke the silence.

"The night you went to prom, your mom and I were laying in bed waiting for you to come home and she kept saying how the next big night like this you would have would be your wedding day," I went on, "She talked about how excited she was to do all the planning with you and find a dress," I told Elena who surprisingly wasn't crying as hard as I thought anymore. She sat there and just listened to me go on and on about her mother. I told her all about things her mother would say about her to let her know really how proud she was of Elena. We laughed, cried, a little bit of everything, and it was just what we both needed.

"Elena, you know how much your mother would have loved to be here with you today," I held her hand tight as her head rested on my shoulder.

"I just wish I could have her for one more day, I needed her for just one more day dad," She said as tears again fell from her face and onto my pants.

Trying to hold back the tears myself, I looked at her as she lifted her head and said, "You know what the right thing to do here is, but whatever you decide to do I will be there with you every step of the way."

She took a deep breath and without saying a thing in response, she turned toward the doors of the hotel and made her way back inside. I followed closely behind feeling a big weight being lifted off my shoulders. On her way back inside, she stopped and grabbed a small handful of the purple mums her mother loved so dearly. She lifted them up to her nose, took a deep breath, and headed towards the door for a second time with the mums in hand.

As I stood behind her upon the opening of the doors to the room filled with agitated and impatient people whose moods immediately got brighter when they laid eyes on Elena, I felt at peace as the sun shined through the windows and lite up the room. I knew that was a sign from Jane but I wasn't sure if Elena had recognized it as she walked down the aisle.

"I do," they both said and audience clapped for what felt like eternity. The justice of the peace proceeded to say, "You may now kiss your bride," and the clapping grew louder. The whole room was cheering, I was cheering, and Jane was definitely cheering. A tear fell down my face and I was finally feeling the joy I was supposed to be feeling for Elena today.

Fruitless Worship

The Great Realm in which I reside in, surrounds my cage, as the children, or as the Chief calls them, children, rush in each day. Tapping my house, the children always speak to me, saying things like "Good morning, Mr. Whiskers!" and "Time to wake up!" They stare into my home in what seems like a mixture of awe and astonishment, as if my very presence enlightens and enhances the rest of their day. The Chief always enters the room a few seconds later, and as I begin to wake up, the children go through their normal routine while the Chief takes a seat at his mighty throne. I do not know what it is that the Children and Chief do within this realm, but it must be important if they have to come here everyday. The chief stands up and passes around some paper for the children to write on.

"We are having a pop quiz today, class!" he says aloud.

The children make many expressions ranging from shock to boredom with the idea of a so called "pop quiz." At first I think it might be that lovely food that the children call popcorn. Sometimes they'll open up the door to my home and throw a few pieces in-that is the best stuff ever; I could eat it for days. The thought that I'd be getting any of that scrumptious food goes out the window as I see the Chief begin to pass out pieces of paper to the Children-there's never any paper needed for popcorn. As he hands each child a paper, they hurriedly begin to write, a child in the front row stands up and shouts "done!" He places the paper by the Chief's throne. This act causes the children to look up quickly, and then they all look back to finishing even faster than anyone else.

Eventually all of the children finish with what was handed out and the Chief looks through the pile. His face changes to a look of disappointment as he holds up one of the pop quizzes with drawings on it that resemble me.

"Charlie, we aren't supposed to make drawings on the quizzes," his voice drops as his eyes look blankly at Charlie with a stare that could burn through paper.

Charlie and the other Children giggle to themselves as the Chief looks up to the time teller on wall. I look over towards Charlie, who has a look of satisfaction mixed with a glint in his eye and a puffed up chest. His little drawing and the annoyance from the teacher earned him some attention from the other students, his little grin couldn't stretch any further than it already was. The Chief then puts a clean version of the "pop quiz" and walks back over to his throne.

"School is almost over, so Charlie you need to actually answer the quiz for me, the rest of you can either work on your homework or wait until the bell rings for dismissal."

A few of the children excitedly leap out of their desks and come to check up on me as well as groom me. One of their large hairless paws slowly glide along my back which creates a slight tingle that goes up through my spine. One of the children also even made sure that the area in which I get my food was well stocked, and by well stocked I mean that he emptied the entire bottle of food pellets into the form of a small hill.

After a while, they all start to leave. A few of the children even decided to stick around to talk to me. The sounds of sad farewells and hope that they will be able to see me tomorrow sweetly travel through my ears like a sweet lullaby.

"See you later, Mr. Whiskers!" says one of the children excitedly, before running out through the gate. Another child pokes at my home before waving to me silently as they walk out. Finally only the Chief and one child remain inside the realm. The Chief pulls the child aside.

"Charlie, today is your turn to take care of Whiskers alright?" the child named Charlie looks towards my home. "Samantha took care of him yesterday, so now it will be your turn to take care of him and to make sure that he will be back here tomorrow, alright?" the Chief said as he rounded the back of his throne where he picked up a massive pile of papers that looked like a mountain scratching at the ceiling.

"Yes sir, I'll make sure to bring him home!" Charlie exclaimed excitedly.

The chief then smiles and begins to go over the "pop-quizzes" and homework that he just pulled out. Charlie picks up his bag and begins to head over to me to bring me to his place of living. As he gets right by my den, he suddenly snaps upwards.

"Oh no, I have to pick up my project from science class, I'll be right back to get you Mr.Whiskers!"

He dashes out of the room without me. I squeak loudly to see if he can hear me and remember the fact that he forget about me. Charlie was supposed to bring me with him to his own home. All of the other children have done this since they were entrusted to take care of me. It was supposed to be Charlie's turn, but instead he had left without me. The Chief was so distracted by the work at his throne, that he didn't even notice that Charlie wasn't doing what he was told. Well I shouldn't worry at all, I mean he did say that he'll come back after all. I mean, he wouldn't forget about me would he?

The lights above have dissipated. The chief left without noticing me after tirelessly trying to get through the mountain of papers he had gone through. At this point, I know that the children and the Chief won't be back for a while. It seems like Charlie has forgotten me or that he is too busy, no matter! The children will be back tomorrow and I will make sure that they will not ever forget me again! With all the time I have to spare in waiting for them, now will be the perfect time to create a gift for them. If I can make the greatest gift for the children, it will surely impress them so that they will never forget about me again. I erect a pile of the soft ground and mold it into a statue that would make even the gods weep with excitement and happiness. All I have to do now is simply wait for the great sun beams to come back and for the children to return.

While crawling into my domain and curling up into a ball, dreams of the children's return spring into mind. Once they come back, I'll show them my statue and win their ever adoring affection! My eyes close and my dreams of being up in the realm that the children call "home" play through my head. I do not know why they like "home" so much, but it is amazing since even the children and the many chiefs like going there all the time. The night soon recedes, as the sun rises from the depths once more.

After crawling out of my den and looking around, I see that none of the Children have arrived yet. No sounds of loud gibberish, no screaming, and no children coming to visit me, tapping on my house. Only silence permeates the surrounding area. They must be taking longer than usual since by now they would have already been here. I have rarely seen them come in at later times, so maybe it is one of those rare days in which I'll have to wait a bit longer than usual. I crawl across the ground of my den and hop into my big wheel. Any pointless thoughts are whisked away which allows for the time around me to flow smoothly and quickly like the water out of the great grey fountains the children drink from. However, My thoughts keep swirling around my fuzzy head. I start to stare out of my home and begin thinking about what to do. A thought suddenly flies into my head that makes me realize that with the children gone, I have to do something. I could simply wait for their return instead of going out and looking for them. That could be a good idea, but the thought of them even coming back for a while seems pointless. The plate of food that was filled to the brim yesterday has only a few bare scraps left on it, like trees in a desert. I'll need to go and find the children in order to get some more food, instead of them coming back to get me and filling up my plate. My whole body flinches at the mere thought of potentially starving. The ground that I sleep on shall be the way to getting out of my domain. I shove and push the very soft earth into the corner of my home. The ground is easy to pull and push as bits and pieces of it begin to slow stack up in a corner of my home. After stacking the earth in my pen, I slowly ascend up the mound where I can feel the soft earth sinking underneath me. The ground sticks to my paws as I keep climbing to reach the top that seems far away. After what feels like an eternity, the top of my home appears before me. This is the first time I have gone out by myself without the children or chief's help.

The area where the children gather is immeasurable to me. This realm in which I live in is a mere gathering area for them. Now it will be a part of a long and arduous journey for me. I'll have to go underneath the thrones of the children and pass the Chief's domain, and make my way to the mighty gate in which the Children go out and in from. The surroundings shall indeed make this trip a harrowing and exhilarating experience! I shall find Charlie and make sure that he won't leave me again. My paws scratch the smooth ground as I move, the land is dark and there is little to no light coming from the clear gates behind me. The sound of me scurrying across the ground echoes throughout the realm. After crawling towards the Great Gate for what feels like a few minutes, I manage to finally get to the Gate. I shove my body against it and try to open the gate. It doesn't budge even a little. I will not be defeated by a mere oversized door! I shove against the crack in the hopes of trying to open the gate. The sound of the gate creaking open can be heard as I feel myself moving along with it. Soon enough, the gate is wide open for me to squeeze through.

The halls are massive and expansive, yet the children traverse these halls casually with not a care in the world. The thought of the sheer size of the things the people make, actually freaks me out a little. I haven't really seen much outside of the school or the children's homes. How big is the world outside from what I have seen?

While thinking about some of these burning questions, silence continues to linger throughout the halls. My journey to find the Children that I worship shall now start. Traveling along the path of the halls makes me wonder. I was so focused on those questions that I had not even noticed the fact that I had bumped into the corner of a wall that is connected to multiple halls. The end of the hall opens up to three different places, one is the place where the children do battle with red balls, another leads to where they gather to feast, and the last one leads to more places where the other Children gather with separate Chiefs. The third hall leads to the exit of this huge place that houses all of these areas. That is where my journey will take me to go find the children.

👁 👁

The exit soon comes into sight after my difficult and strenuous journey which leads to me finding that the outside is brighter than ever. It is bright white with a lot of reflections on the ground, and the trees have white fluff covering them, like a coat of soft fur. My eyes can't look for too long before they dry up and sting. From what I could see, no one is here. The gates that lead outside are huge and can't be moved like the previous gate I had encountered. With the revelation of what the gates and outside look like, waiting for the Children to return sounds like a better idea than trying to escape out of here.

Suddenly a sound occurs from behind that causes me to turn around to see a mop that oozes out a dirty slime. It sweeps towards me and I have to run into a corner to avoid it. It misses me and sweeps forward at where I was previously. I peer up to see the Groundskeeper himself, going about and clearing the area. Surely his mop would have harmed me if I had not noticed him behind me. The Groundskeeper never really showed me any attention in the past and it seemed like he could care less about me, unlike the children. There has to be some Children lingering about if the Groundskeeper is here.

👁 👁

The Groundskeeper is slowly moving through the halls. I go in the opposite direction of him and go in search of a way to open the front gates. There must be some sort of key or object I can use to open it so that I can find the children. The Groundskeeper finishes his sweep and begins to head back towards me. Something needs to happen, in order for me to get past him. That moment soon becomes clear when he leans

50

over to pick up a piece of discarded piece of paper. I get behind him and move onward to look for keys. Soon another new area lays before me that is unfamiliar. This area seems familiar to the one I live in. It looks the same, except I can clearly see another den that has some sort of scaled beast in it. It stares at me and doesn't bother to blink at all. There is a large piece of sticky paper plastered up on the upper right hand corner of its home. It has the words "Mr.Silky" on it which reveals to me this creature's name. The beast quickly crawls along the numerous sticks it has in its home, all the while it pumps its head up and down. It even puffs up it's chin that is a deep shade of orange. The Children in this area probably love the erratic behaviour of this creature. My thoughts aren't entertained any further as I feel myself being squeezed and lifted upwards. I see that the Groundskeeper has found me wandering around his domain.

He moves his mouth and speaks in a low grunting voice, the soft rumbles coming from his mouth make it hard to even understand him. After his talk he turns around and the sound of jingling occurs as he moves forward. I peer down to his side to see what looks like a large assortment of keys that the Groundskeeper uses to open the gates. He turns and starts moving towards his mop. I don't want to be taken back yet before finding out why the Children have not arrived yet! My mouth clamps down on the Groundskeeper's finger in hopes of him releasing me. He flinches and drops me, the moment of my fall down slows down to a crawl. The groundskeeper's keys are right beneath me, I edge out enough in order to snap onto the ring. The second I touch the keys, time immediately catches up. My weight causes the keys to fall, along with me, onto the mop which comforts my drop. I drag the keys towards the gate in order to leave. However, the Great Gates don't open. No matter how much I try to wedge the key into the gap, they simply will not budge. Once again, I feel the Groundskeeper's hand grab a hold of me. The Groundskeeper brings me towards my home and places me back inside it, effectively restarting my journey. The Groundskeeper has just put a major halt on my plans of finding any of the children. I shuffle and crawl into my sleeping space and I promptly pass out from the exhausting adventure I had just gone on.

My questions as to why the Children have not come back to me yet have not been answered. A whole day has gone by of waiting for them to return. It has gotten to a point where I consumed all of my snacks and water. Suddenly, I hear voices coming from afar. The children must have returned! At least, I think they did as big balls of fluff waddle into the room. The Great Chief has appeared but I do not understand why the Children are wearing such big coats of fur. I did not even know that they could grow that much fur! The Great Chief says something and the other children take off their coats of fur in a few seconds. I couldn't even do that, and if I tried I would just shed a few hairs at most. The Children have white fluff on their coats and in that moment I realize why the Children took so long to get back. They must have taken time getting through all of that weird white stuff outside that reflects the sun that I saw beforehand when I passed by the main gates. Soon the children all go through the day doing their tasks and work they were assigned and soon get ready to leave once more. Now that I know that the Children need to take time to get to this realm due to the natural forces outside, a few of my concerns are put to rest. Now that they have come back, I realize that being alone for a little while isn't too bad. Charlie even came up to my home in shock due to the fact that he had forgotten about me this whole time! He looks at me and then at my empty food bowl. He looks towards the chief and then back to me. His eyes show signs of sadness and he promptly adds some more food to my bowl. He then walks over to the chief and starts to talk about how he forgot about me this whole time that they were away. The chief looks to me and then says "Just don't forgot him again alright?" Charlie looks towards me and nods his head with a look of acknowledgement of how he won't try to ever forget about the Guinea pig named Mr. Whiskers.

Looking Through the Glass

Fog blanketed the dark cobblestone streets of Germany, ebbing and flowing through the shops that sat nestled and still in the dead of night. The street lamps flickered on, providing a dim light in the midst of a great shadow. A sudden "crack" was heard in the distance as muffled screams broke the silence and commotion began to fill the desolate evening. A dog barked as a few lights above the shops turned on, illuminating a blood red banner with a crooked black symbol flapping proudly above one of the shops in the crisp fall breeze. Sharp shouting could be heard as men rounded the corner of the street, the urge in their footsteps starkly apparent. The men filling the streets stood in tan uniforms, standing out from the police, carrying long wooden sticks in their hands. Large metal chunks began flying overhead, dropping rocks of fire to the ground and making everything rumble. Vehicles raided the streets, making the inside of the stores shake. In one store, hats fell to the ground from their shelves and hooks. Small pieces of my body began to fall to the ground, hitting the sidewalk crumpling on impact. Despite the chaos that seemingly took over the street that night, the sudden activity wasn't how it always was on our street.

Despite all of the traffic, the neighborhood was filled with a sense of playful charm during the daylight hours. Children filled the streets playing games, and the familiar neighbors commuted to work every day. In weeks past, those bustling streets seemed busy no more, and the neighborhood became very quiet. No more did children come up and look through me or play games on the sidewalks. All of this left me with one question- where were the people going?

⟨ ⟩ ⟨ ⟩

Each day as the sun would start to rise above the tops of the trees, the shadow of a man who I'd grown quite fond of, would make his way down the street each morning. Every day that same man, the owner of the hat shop, would wear his brown hat with a circular brim that came to a precise point.

Things were not as they'd always been in Germany or, as people were calling it now, the Motherland. Everything was changing and as it did, uncertainty seemed to be the only thing that was constant.

He would start his day picking up any rumble from me that may have fallen outside the shop, always saying the same line through deep sighs "can't have kids getting cut on glass". The click clack of the lock and the spring of an open door was a routine that persisted every day except for Saturdays because of the Sabbath. The shop owner would start his day as the sun was rising. Each day, he would use some liquid and a rag and rub it all over me, which tickled. Out of routine, he'd arrange the rows of hats standing behind me that were displayed to the public, paying particular attention to the ones on the mannequins. When everything was to his liking, he'd enter the back room to cut all the leather and materials for the orders that he had to fill. In those wee hours of the morning and late into the evening, the hat maker would create his best works of art, and as he finished each one, he'd place it on a pedestal, allowing me to showcase his masterpieces to the world.

Each hat was particular and unique to the person who ordered it. Only the finest leather from faraway lands was used to craft these personal masterpieces. He took great pride in his work- every stitch and seam needed to be just right. The hat maker's most prized possession was the hat he wore each day. Crafted with great precision and care, his hat stood out from all of the others. The hat was brown leather, which was stitched with a smooth seam, invisible to the eye. A frail gold ribbon was wrapped around the chocolate brown hat that represented the fashionable look that the owner always had. His passion even seemed to spill into his mistakes. On more than one oc-casion, if a stitch came out wrong or a seam ran crooked, he'd become noticeably frustrated, often taking the hat and throwing it away, each time saying to himself how his customers expected perfection. The recurring punch of the sewing machine was so repetitive and yet, it provided such a comforting sound. The door opened and the little bell would ring, echoing into my old wooden walls that lined that very back of the shop and the sewing machine would cease. The hat maker would come out from the back, wearing a leather apron that he'd crafted. "Hello there," he would say to his customers, "How can I help you today?" in his light and cheery tone. He would start off by stretching a tape measure in his artisan hands with great delicacy, as the measure began to wrap around each of his customer's head. All kinds of interesting people bought hats from the hat maker-businessmen, mothers, soldiers, bakers, bankers, and even the poor saved up enough green paper to purchase a hat from one of the best hat makers in Germany. Despite his great work and acclaimed fame with the townspeople, it wasn't enough to sustain a living once the men began patrolling the streets. The shopkeeper often referred to them as "Nazis" and it seemed as each day passed, his worry about them grew stronger.

At first, these men would only walk by the shop. I'd see them tell children to slow down or tell someone to pay attention to where they were walking. But as time went by, they seemed to grow very mean. Walking along the sidewalk, they would gaze through me, into the shop with angry, snarling faces, watching every move the hat maker made. Women who walked by would cover their children's eyes as they hastened their step, and working men, many of whom I'd seen in the shop before, began to shout nasty names like "filthy Jew" or "money monger" at me.

One day a man dressed in a dark pinstriped suit entered the shop. He began yelling all kinds of names at the owner. He bossed the owner around ordering him to make him a hat. "You filthy Jew, I want you to make me a hat for free" the owner refused. The owner refused and asked the man to leave. The customer knocked down shelves and the hats that sat atop them. The man in the suit charged the owner reaching for the prized hat. Ripping the hat off of the man's head he threw it to the ground and planted his heel through the hat. He then stormed out of the shop, causing a great scene.

Yet, through all of this, the shopkeeper seemed to only pay mind to his business and kept doing what he did best- maybe the shopkeeper could not hear, or maybe he was too focused on his work to care.

I don't know why they called the shopkeeper filthy. He never looked filthy-the clothes he wore always were neatly pressed, mirroring the precision and look of the hats he'd made himself. There was nothing filthy about the way he looked. In fact, he often looked better than the people passing by, making the comments.

As the days passed, there was a tension that began to grow-children no longer filled the streets to play; they were now always accompanied by adults and seemed to be in a rush to get somewhere.

The shopkeeper would come in, sitting at the front desk with his face buried in his hands. One morning his routine changed instead of coming in and organizing the shop to prepare for the day ahead he locked the door behind him. The owner took off his suit jacket and placed it a top the counter. The owner disappeared in the back only to return with a sewing kit and a yellow star. Crystal tears began to well up in his eyes as the man stitched that yellow star onto his sleeve.

The weeks and days seemed to drag on and business seems to slow. No longer was the shop filled with laughter and happy customers. At the end of each day, the man began to count the green bundle of paper and slip it from the big metal box into a hole inside his shirt pocket. But the paper seemed to disappear over the course of these weeks. The punch of the sewing machine stopped and the same hats sat on the shelf collecting dust and the man adapted to this new routine.

The bell on the door jingled for the last time as the clicking of the lock filled the empty store. The luminescent glow of the moon projected through me onto the wooden floors. The street outside was quiet, but the eerie calm did not last very long. The whines of those metal chunks flew overhead into the night sky. The low, steady rumble of thunder shook the city. Dogs barked and men yelled as shrieks of terror rang out through the night.

It then happened. Men in dark uniforms filled the street, words spat out of mouths full of disgust. With a quick flash of a bat, I finally knew pain. As the wood connected with my body, shard and shatter. I had never felt so uncovered or bare in my entire life. The men stepped on my body that speckled the ground. The cash register was drained, the hats were stolen, very little remained. One of the uniformed men slapped some colored liquid with a brush on me, that tickled just like the old man had done. The lines made up that crooked symbol that was on all of the flags and uniforms. From behind me, I could feel an intense heat growing and growing. Flashes of red light erupted through me. I wanted to scream, but I had no way of doing so. Why were these men doing this to me? What made them choose me and this shop? Where was the owner? The men moved on to the next building and a man in uniform took out a paint can and brushed red paint on its remains. The embers burned harshly for the rest of the evening and eventually died out in the early hours of the morning.

Uniformed men sat outside the shop resting their tired eyes, some patrolling the street for trouble. A familiar shadow of a man turned the corner and walked down the sidewalk. The man picked up his pace and began flailing with commotion. The men in uniform sprung up, preparing to take on the heckler. Drawing his wooden bat, the soldier raised the club above the owner. With a great pull of strength the uniformed man slashed the helpless hat man. A crack echoed off the cold street as the bat connected with his rib cage. His eyes began to roll, and a look of horror drowned over him as red liquid trickled onto the sidewalk. The uniformed men began laughing at the shop owner that was now nothing more than a heap on the ground. Their laughter broke as the sound of a truck grew louder until I saw two headlights pull directly in front of me.

Why would they do something so cruel to a man who shared his shared his artwork with the community. The shop owner lay on the sidewalk, crying out in agony and the uniformed men did nothing to help. Wasn't their job to help him? Was the man a criminal- did he do something wrong? Maybe that's why they weren't coming to his aid. But he man didn't deserve to die. In that moment everything seemed unknown. Until one of the men opened their mouth, and the pieces of the puzzle came together. Calling the man a filthy Jew, the man in uniform planted a kick to the shop owner's rib cage. Curling into a ball, the man let out a muffled cry.

As the truck came to a halt, more uniformed men sprung from the truck and stood over the helpless owner. With a swift wind, he kicked the man in the gut again but this time not cry came from the shop owner. Instead, in what looked like a desperate attempt, the man began to grab at the cobblestones with his remaining strength, and that familiar face looked up at the men standing over him. The strength and determination I had one seen in his eyes so many times as he leaned over his workbench was now gone, replaced with a helpless look of sadness. Opening his mouth, he asked the question I'd been asking myself: "why me?" Even in his feeble voice, the words bounced off the empty streets and sleeping buildings. Two of the strange men grabbed the old man, paying no mind to what he'd just asked them. Turning towards me, he took one last look in at his shop, gazing right through me. My remaining pieces stood helpless, and the old man, my friend, began to sob as he was dragged to the back of the truck.

Picking the shop owner up, the uniformed men heaved him into the black hole that was the truck and slammed its door shut. And just like that, the ground began to shake and jet black smoke filled the air as it lurched forwards and slowly crept across the stone cobbled street and into the night, the warm glow of the tail lights quickly fading into darkness. A light snow began to fall; once again all was calm, and just as it had been earlier that evening except for one thing- a familiar circular brimmed shadow and pointed top, once donned by the shop owner, sat motionless awaiting a new head to adorn.

Home

U gh, where is it?" The quick and constant banging on the front door startled me. It's that time of day again. That ear piercing noise is the grumpy store owner screaming at the front door because he can't find his keys, as usual. "Crap! Not again... This happens every day, man." *Same issue different day; check your back pocket, it's always there, buddy.* I wish I knew his name. He must be more than a pissed off man who screams at his employees for not stocking the shelves correctly. Looking through my clear screen, I tried to look for his nametag. All the workers had tags on their shirts: there's Amy, Sam, Lindsey, and more. Their names aren't the ones that matter though- the only name that matters to me is my owner.

"Mommy, Mommy look at this! I want to take him home," screamed a little girl. *Home? That's somewhere I want to go.* My head tilted to the side. This is a place that I always hear, but can never see. Watching other toys being ripped off the shelves confuses me as to where they go. One minute the toys are neatly placed one in front of another and the next, the dusty white shelf is bare. The little girl began to viciously shake my box. My eyes ricocheted back and forth, paws landing on my tail multiple times, teeth sinking into my tongue as my head thumped the top of the box. . *Put me down right now! You're giving me a headache; don't you know this is animal abuse?*

"Why do you want this one? Look at the pink one sweetie, she's your favorite color," she said to her daughter.

Instantly, I was dropped to the floor, and run over by an extremely hyper toddler. She dropped me so hard, my paw hit the corner of my box; I automatically let out a "bark." *Ouch!* In my head I told her to watch out, but that didn't seem to make the situation better seeing that she cannot hear me. *And what do you mean the pink is better? What's wrong with me?. I come with my own toys, a tennis ball and a bone, and I'm famous.* I always see myself on the big screens in the store. I can't make out what they're saying, but the kids seem like they're having a great time laughing and playing fetch with me. It's funny though, I don't remember that day. The only time a human has put their hands on me and not just my box was back at the factory. The man rolled out pieces of my plush fabric on an industrial board. Above me, stood a saw that stitched all of my pieces together. To the side there were a pile of flat plush puppies that looked just like me. The man brought us over to a cylinder shaped machine that was jammed into our heads. Once the machine impaled my skull, a piercing, ear-splitting noise overwhelmed the factory. My whole body went from flat fluff to a full sewn stuffed dog. After that, I was locked up in a sealed box. I laid on the floor helpless, watching them walk away thrilled with their new prized possession. *Way to get my hopes up.*

The store owner called all the employees to the front. "Alright guys, It's going to be a busy night. There will be no time for screwing around and looking miserable."

Every single workers eyes rolled in the back of their heads, arms crossed, putting all their weight on one side, mumbling complaints under their breath.

"1,2,3, testing," someone yelled from the back of my aisle. Bright colored lights illuminated the entire store. Red, blue, green, and yellow created a glare on the walls and other toy boxes. *Why does the store look different today? The green monsters with shiny tennis balls need to be tied up better, guys. That fuzzy string isn't going to hold them back!*

Amy and Lindsey were hanging a sign from the wall.

"Amy, that's not how you do it!"

"How about you step up on the ladder and do it yourself." A half-hung poster drooped down from the brick wall.

Black Friday...Since when do days have colors?

"I should be home right now eating with family, not doing this bullshit," Lindsey said. Amy gave her a smirk and walked away, twirling her long blonde locks.

"Let 'em in!" a voice screamed. An army of people with carts sprinted through the double doors. *Someone's going to get hurt, slow down!* They raced down my aisle, shoving one another. *Man, you give a day of the week a color, and people start acting like rabid animals.* They all continued rolling down the store. *Slow down, pick me!* No one turned around and no one questioned who was screaming at them. Without a care in the world, they just kept moving as though I meant nothing. All their lists had every toy imaginable, except me. Out of anger, I stomped my left paw and three barks left my mouth uncontrollably- I am reminded of the fact that no one can hear me.

The shelf across from mine was almost bare. Turns out Headbands is the most popular item in the store seeing that there is only one left.

"Great, the last one!" The man reached over his cart to put the game in his empty cart.

"Hey! I was just coming over here to get that," hollered another man zipping through the aisle. As he turned his cart, the wheels against the tiles created an ear piercing noise. His cart veered to the right side, moving on two wheels, almost flipping over.

"Man, leave me alone. I got here first; it's for my kids now get out of my way." As he pushed his cart forward to leave the aisle the hostile man grabbed the game. Like immature four year olds, the two grown men held tightly onto each side of the box, grasping it so hard that the corns started to wrinkle and cave in. The cardboard box tore apart, 72 cards exploded in the air falling to the floor like confetti. The timer smashed open once it hit the floor, spilling the sand right in front of me. My tail slowly moved between my legs, ears flopped down, and snout pointed at my paws. *I've never realized how sensitive dog ears are, I need to go home.*

A familiar face strolled in across from me. She was holding a long white thin piece of paper, and walked with the employee Sam.

"Found the spot, it goes right here," said Sam, tossing the pink dog back on the shelf.

"Thank you! After I bought it, my daughter realized she'd have more fun with the play dough set." *Hey pink dog, how are you still smiling? You were just returned to the shelves! You got to see your new home and everything. What a tease. I wouldn't be smiling if I were you.*

"Dear Santa, the first thing I want is the stuffed brown dog that barks," Mumbled a tall blonde woman standing above me holding a "Christmas list." The corners of a Crayola box impaled my screen as I was shoved into a pact cart. Not once has my body been able to feel being pushed miles per hour throughout the store. The wind against my body made my eyes and ears stretch to the back of my head. My bushy tail wags 100 miles per hour, and my floppy ears stood high as I turned my head from all of the excitement. *This means someone is officially buying me. I'm going to belong to someone, finally. I can't wait to see what home looks like.* I felt so much excitement that my tongue began to leave my mouth as I panted.

As the car came to an abrupt stop, I slid out of the bag with my face pressed up against a clear window. A small green store caught my eye immediately. *Where are all the shelves, and other toys?*

"Tom, I'm home," whispered the woman.

"Okay, I'll bring out the wrapping paper, Stacey," said Tom. A long tube of green and red shiny paper with snowflakes covered me completely. *I can't even see what is around me anymore! I want to be played with, not decorated.*

"See you again in a month," said Stacey. Coldness blew through the damp space I was put in. Just like a misplaced toy put on the wrong shelf, I was all alone- isolated from everyone who was the same as that specific toy. Every little creek that came from god knows where echoed through the room. *I can't believe I'm thinking this, but I wish I was back on the shelves. I may not have been the one for anyone except now, but the kids faces were priceless.*

One time, a man was holding a baby and her head rested on his shoulder as he whispered "shh" in her ear. Every time she looked over at the at me, she gave a faint smile and stopped crying. *That day he didn't even thank me for getting his whiny child to quiet down...What a jerk.*

The sound of screaming startled me. All I can see is black darkness. Motions from stomping made my stomach turn as it came closer and closer. As I'm being ripped open, a huge smile and beating eyes met me at eye level.

"Look what Santa got me, Mommy!" screamed a little girl.

"See Abby, I told you Santa would know exactly what you wanted!" said Stacey.

This demon child was squeezing me so hard, I thought she was going to break my battery paw. *I can't breathe you need to let go before stuffing pops out of my stitches.*

"I'm going to go play with her now," she said. *Her? Don't you know I'm a man? Look at my blue collar; if you wanted the girl, you should have asked for the pink one.*

"Abby, you have more presents to open up," said Tom.

"But I'm going to play with her now!" demanded Abby. She pulled me by the collar, and dragged me into her room. Abby placed me on a hard white chair surrounding other stuffed animals. "This is my new puppy everyone! I don't have a name yet, but she'll be playing with us from now on." *Does she know they can't talk? They're all just staring blankly at the wall. Maybe they're just scared of a big famous dog like me.*

Abby plopped herself on the couch next to me; my body started slowly moving into the crack in the couch. Her innocent eyes were glued to the TV, not even realizing that I'm in trouble. *A little help, Abby?* Crumbs from her obnoxiously chewing goldfish were covering my head. *You know, I'm not your trash can.*

"Abby, time to eat," yelled Tom. Abby flew off the couch faster than the grumpy store owner could scream at his employees the second they screwed up, and trust me, he didn't miss any mess ups in that place. *Wait! You're forgetting me... This doesn't feel right. I get to eat with them every night!* 6 o'clock sharp I sit at the head of the table jealously watching them devour what is on their plates. "Do you want to go meet mom for some ice cream?" asked Tom. Abby's eyes lit up as bright as the colored lights in the store.

"Yes!" she screamed as she kicked her legs.

Good thing were going out for dessert, you owe me one. Abby and Tom put on their jackets, and Abby picked me up. *Abby, you just passed the front door, back up!* She opened her bedroom door and tried throwing me onto her bed, but four year olds dont have the best aim. I hit the bed frame, and landed into a pile of dress up clothes in a box. The right corner of the box hit my paw. The stitching in my paw tore allowing fluffy stuffing to pop out, making my left side look flat. *Great, a rip.*

The light from the car shined through the window. I could see how excited they were to leave without me. *How could I go from being everything to nothing in just one day? Lately, I guess, I haven't been treated right.* I waited for them to come home for what felt like hours. *Why am I not good enough?*

I woke up to the sound of laughter. My tail shot up and I looked out the window towards the patio. Abby was on top of Stacey's shoulders with her arms flying through the air. *Time to play!* She skipped into her room holding a snow white fluffy polar bear.

"I won the crane game! I won the crane game!" Abby sang happily. She shoved all her books and toys off her circle table, and plopped down her new prized possession; her eyes bulged out of her head as she smiled widely at it. Her head rested perfectly between her two hands as she tilted her head back and forth, and softly sang her song. *She didn't even say hi to me when she walked in.* The rip in my leg began to pour out white fluffy stuffing, but it's nothing that she can see. I'm not a priority anymore. I can sit here all night losing fluff, and no one would notice. *I guess this is how it feels to be replaced. I'm officially just like that pink dog, except I'm not still smiling...Well at least on the inside.*

"Abby tomorrow morning we're packing up toys you don't like anymore. This house has too many toys lying around that you don't use," said Stacey as she threw two garbage bags by the door.

Yeah thats right! Throw everything out, besides me of course, including that eye sore on the table. As Abby hopped onto her bed, she stepped on my paw, "bark!" She grabbed me by the leash, and stared deeply in my eyes. *Yeah, remember me?* Shrugging her shoulders, Abby threw me back down on the ground, bringing the polar bear into bed with her.

I felt myself being suffocated as I was crowded with other toys contained in one area. My snout was deeply pressed up against what seems like white plastic. *Someone get me out and untwist my body; I can't bare this pain anymore. And while you're at it, unhook my leash, I can't breathe.* Dust that coated my body found its way into my mouth as I was gasping for air. I tried kicking the loose Lego pieces away from under my paws, but they weren't going anywhere. *Where am I?* Every sharp turn that was made, my head slid into the buttons of a toy phone, making it say numbers out loud.

"7,9,8,7,9,8," it repeatedly shouted with obnoxious music playing in the background to the tune of the numbers.

"Finally here," said Stacey to herself. My vision is too foggy to see what is around me. *I can't believe Abby is getting rid of me after all this time. Man just put me back on the shelves, please.* An older woman with glasses opened the door. Her back was hunched over, and she was holding a stick. Her hair was neatly wrapped up on the top of her head- not one piece was sticking out.

"Come on in! Just place the bag down right there." She pointed to the middle of a play room. Ten small children looked down at me and the rest of the toys in awe. *You can't keep me here! It smells like wet dog.* The kid's hair was a raggedy mess. Hair strands stuck out left and right. What looks like dirt, covered two kids faces, but they didn't seem to care. Their pants had huge rips revealing scars on their knee caps. All at once, they ripped open the bag. It's like a volcano exploded- we went everywhere. The kids ran around the room, some even had eyes filled with tears.

"Thank you so much!" they all yelled at once basically tackling Stacey to the ground.

"Lets all play with this one together," said one of the girls. All ten of them laid down on the dirty floor petting my soft fur.

I'm home.

Found You

Bright flashes of lights blinded my eyes as I was forced into the dark room. Two police officers walked me in, holding my arms as though I was about to make a run for it. Sitting at the table was an FBI agent. He was giving me a look of disappointment-almost the same look my parents used to give me when I would let them down in countless ways they never forgot to mention.

"So, why'd you do it, huh? Are you some psychopath who wants to scare families, innocent families?" whaled Harrison.

Light splashes of spit hit my face as he met me at eye level. The smell of coffee in his breath pervaded my nose as he began pacing back and forth behind me, knuckles clenched, rubbing his hands over one another, the whole time eyes deadlocked on me.

"Ha! Innocent my ass. You don't know me or my situation," I laughed, fiddling with my fingers, lifting my handcuffed hands off the cold metal table. "Wanna take these off me man? I'm getting sore."

Harrison slowly paced around the room, tapping his pen on his lip, gazing at the ceiling.

"Tell me about the first scene," he said, ignoring my request, his eyes bugged out of his head, curious as to what was going on in my brain. With a pen in his hand, he was ready to write my statement. Like I was going to tell him everything. I turned my cheek, spit on the floor, and gave him a smile back. "Seriously? Do you think this is a joke?" The outside of Harrison's face showed amusement, but the inside was definitely the opposite. I could see right through his eyes- he just wanted to remain professional, like any agent would; he's disgusted with my actions..

"First scene? How is that any of your business? Nothing I did was wrong."

Harrison punched the wall and kicked the rolling chair across from me. Scabs on his knuckles tore, allowing blood to form on his hand, dripping down his fingers.

"And I'm the one who's psycho?" I asked looking him up and down. He began tugging the ends of his hair as he walked back to the seat.

"You know Andrew, when people have difficulty answering a simple question, most of the time it means they're guilty," Harrison said, covering his mouth with his hand.

I sunk in my chair, squeezing my fists, wishing I wasn't incapable of maneuvering my hands. What I would do to whack that childish smirk off his face.

"Andrew, we already caught you. You might as well just tell us what happened," Harrison said in distress. Four hours of trying to get me to talk were starting to show on his face; dark bags now began to line his eyes.

"I'm not telling you fools anything."

Harrison reached across the table, tightening my handcuffs.

"Just pretend like it doesn't bother you," I said to myself. I couldn't give him the satisfaction of seeing me get worked up. I sat back in my chair, tapping my fingers. The sound of nails repeatedly hitting a hard surface gave me some sort of comfort, making me forget about the fact that these cuffs were cutting off the circulation in my wrists. "I'd rather play a game. Let's see how much longer I can keep you cowards wasting your time on something that wasn't even a crime," I screamed out of irritation, smashing both my fists on the table.

Again, Harrison made the handcuffs stiffer. The creases in his forehead were visible, eyebrows pointed directly above his nose, waiting for me to surrender.

"Enough!" I screamed, clenching my fists.

"Well, you see, I don't play games. Keep screwing around and you'll see where you're going to end up next," stressed Harrison. I continued to tap my nails against the table. "If you don't start talking, we're through here, and I'm just going to have you locked up. I don't care whether or not I have a confession from you, you're guilty! No one was seen with the kid except for you." He pressed the cuffs together as tight as they'd go, the cold steel began digging into my wrists, all the while he was smiling like a child who was winning some sort of game.

"I guess I can talk now. I want to get home just as much as you do, Adam," I said, looking up at the clock that now read 4:25.

"That's Harrison to you," he said, pointing directly at me. "And you're funny if that's where you think you're going after this." He took a seat across from me with pen and paper, and began to loosen up the cuffs.

"I saw him at a park. Silver Springs State Park, to be exact. He was running up and down a trail, but didn't seem happy. It was as though he was missing something. That something was me." Looking up, I gave him a death stare; glaring as deeply as I could into his hazel eyes.

"You just grabbed a random child away fro-"

"If you want me to talk, quit interrupting me. As I was saying, he looked depressed. His mom was walking slowly behind him, not even paying attention to what he was doing. That careless woman was walking aimlessly glued to her phone. I was hiding behind a tree watching him. My foot slipped while I tried to get a better view of the kid." My palms soaked in sweat as my eyes looked up at Harrison. Again, he was giving me that look of disappointment. "Branches on the ground snapped in half, which caught his attention. He yelled out to his mom, 'I hear an animal, mommy! Come here!' And guess what she did? She stood in place and continued texting, or whatever she was doing. He ran from tree to tree looking for some sort of animal. His foot got caught in a pile of sticks, and I realized that was my perfect moment. I wasn't actually planning on taking him. I just saw it as my chance to start my life again. He thought I was going to help get his foot loose, as I ran towards him, but I covered his mouth and took off with him in my hands."

"In your screwed up head that gave you the right to take a child that doesn't belong to you?" Harrison asked, waving his hands in the air.

I'm not even going to bother answering that question- I'm not a criminal. If he only knew the truth.

"I'm back from the grocery store!" Natalie's voice echoed through our box-sized apartment. "I could use some help."

"Busy," I responded, flipping through the TV channels on the couch.

"Come on, I have ten more bags in the car. You won't get up because you're 'busy' watching nothing?" she snapped. I whipped my head to my left side, where she was hovering over me.

"If you put bags in the trunk, then you're sure as hell capable of taking the same bags out of there."

"Just because you lost your job, doesn't make it right to be a jerk. Get off the couch and stop drinking. Your eyes are the same color as that merlot in the kitchen."

Her arms crossed over her body, waiting for me to attend to her needs.

"Wow. Someone is finally sticking up for herself." Stumbling off the sofa, I shoved her to the side and put my last paycheck into the safe. "When you're done moping around, I'll take some dinner. It's like 6 o'clock, I'm hungry."

She walked out of the room, wiping a single tear running down her cheek. Slamming the door shut behind her, she walked back down towards the car. Through the window, I watched her struggling to walk back inside with the groceries. She looked like a little girl walking across a balance beam for the first time in gymnastics- swaying side to side, arms flailing.

Natalie slouched in her chair, twirling her spaghetti, resting her head on her fist.

"You gonna eat?" I asked as I was obnoxiously slurping my food, shoving it down my throat as though is was going to go somewhere.

"Not hungry," she responded, looking up from the food. Natalie's eyes quickly moved back down at her full plate that was now cold.

"Wanna tell me what's wrong?" I threw my fork down in my plate. The sound of stainless steel smacking glass rang through my ears.

"It's just that...Well...You know, we've only been married three months and I feel like I already can't take it anymore," her eyes retreated back to her plate

"Well guess what? I can't take anymore of your constant complaining. I'm ready to start a family, and I'm so sick of you acting like you don't care."

"I'm the one who doesn't care?!" she snarled. Taken back, she threw her napkin down on her full plate and stormed out of the kitchen.

"You know, you wouldn't be this depressed if we started a family," I said to Natalie. I walked over to the bed where she was curled up in a ball crying. She lifted her head from her knees, and her face looked like a raccoon. Mascara was embedded under her eyes, and a few lines of black were smeared on her cheeks- her white shirt became stained with light orange makeup as tears fell from her face.

"Depressed? You think that's what's wrong with me?"

"Just think about it! Our first boy will be named Jake, and if we have a girl, her name will be Olivia!" I said with excitement.

"Oh my God, you're insane! Get the hell out of here, now!"

Book corners hit my eyes, pens were thrown at my face like darts, and even an empty beer bottle from the night before hit my shoulder and shattered. With rage, I stormed into the bathroom to clean myself up. Microscopic pieces of shattered glass stuck to the sleeves of my shirt. Just below my right eye was scratched. I watched blood run down my face as I stood in front of the mirror, dabbing a wet cloth on it.

The pain of the glass shards cutting into my hand was unbearable. Whipping the closet door open, my hands began swatting everything off the shelves, looking for a pair of tweezers. "Come on, where are they?!" I slid my hand across the middle shelf, knocking useless lotions and perfume bottles on the tile floor. "Finally." The tweezers rested in the corner of the almost empty shelf. Biting down on a towel, I used them to pull the pieces of glass out of my skin.

"Hope you calmed down, because I'm coming back in." Natalie positioned herself in the corner of the bed, laying completely still, eyes wide open, not saying one word. "If you're going to act like a brat, just go to bed." Immediately, her arm shot up and turned the light switch off. Disgusted with her behavior, I slept in the spare bedroom for the night.

"Natalie, I'm up!" I yelled, my voice echoing through the apartment. There was no answer. Normally, breakfast in bed would be brought straight to me once I woke up. "Natalie!" I hollered even louder this time, and still no response. I sprung out of bed to see what she was up to. "Probably watching T.V. or something," I mumbled to myself. The door leading to the hallway stairs outside of our apartment was cracked open. "Is someone in here? Come on Natalie, this isn't funny." The safe next to the T.V. was wide open too. My drunk self completely forgot to lock the damn safe. I slammed it shut in rage. Just the thought of money alone took control of my head. All my money, gone. Social security card, passport, wallet, license, disappeared.

"Are you kidding me?" I was pacing back and forth around the room, making my head spin. Chair legs were snapped in half underneath the kitchen table, and the seats were all flipped over. "This can't be happening. This isn't real," I said as I went to the bathroom to splash water on my face in hopes it would wake me up from this nightmare.

Brown, long locks covered the sink drain. A pair of scissors sat in the corner of the bathroom floor, next to a diamond ring. I looked at myself in the mirror, grasping the sink tightly, and my face scrunched up.

"I am going to find you."

"Answer me!" demanded Harrison. He sprang up from the chair, making it roll to the back of the room, smashing into the wall. Both fists violently hit the table. I was able to feel the vibrations straight through my arms. "Did that give you the right to steal someone else's child, yes or no?"

"Right, someone else's child." Grinning at him, I shrugged my shoulders. Veins in his neck were sticking out like a sore thumb. Struggling to keep his cool, Harrison calmly said, "Okay, let's just move on to a new question. So, what happened with the car accident?"

"Flipped the car; you already know that."

"I just need you to tell the full story, Andrew. No need to get up-tight," Drops of sweat trickled down his forehead as his hands were shaking aggressively.

"You seem tense; I think I've given you enough information at this point." His hands grabbed mine, and I quickly pulled away before he tightened those chains back up. "Okay, okay, okay! After I grabbed the kid, I started to panic. There were probably cameras somewhere in the parking lot. I couldn't get into my car."

"Couldn't get into his own car," Harrison mumbled as his hand scribbled across the paper. The only readable words were "car, panic, and child."

"He was in my arms the whole time as I sprinted down the trail. The park was surprisingly empty for a Saturday afternoon. I'm not really sure where, but there was a smaller parking lot towards the end of the trail. Two or three cars were parked there. I yanked all the car doors, and luckily, one car was unlocked." Harrison sat back in his chair, arms crossed, biting down on his lip. "When I was a teenager, my buddies and I learned how to hotwire cars. I bypassed the ignition system, and drove straight onto the highway. There was no destination in mind; I just had to go somewhere, ya know?"

"What was the child doing at this point?" asked Harrison.

"I'm getting to that. The kid was in the back seat. I asked him to keep his head down in case we were being followed. He was crying and screaming, 'I want my mommy' and 'I want to go home.' I was fed up, so I took my eyes off the road. I whipped my head around, screaming at him. 'Shut up, Jake! Just shut up!' He cried back, 'that's not my name.' My foot was still on the gas pedal, eyes focused on the child, it felt as though everything was closing in on me; I stared blankly at him, confused."

"I don't get it. Why is it an issue that his name isn't Jake?" He began giving me a bewildered look, as I shook my head laughing.

"Let me get back to the story. His mouth opened widely, and his eyes focused on the windshield. Next thing I knew, my airbags shot out. My head spun around, and the car was flipping over the guardrail. We were upside down; I truly didn't even know what was going on, or what to do. There was no way out of this situation. I knew police were going to rush to the scene. Whether I called them or someone else driving did, I was going to get caught."

"Alright Andrew, we have enough information. If you don't mind, the mother of the child, Amy, wants to see you."

"Perfect. Let her in," I said smirking back at him.

A woman, with now short, dirty blonde hair, walked slowly through the door. She was more attractive with the dark, long hair. Looking at her, the same feeling I got when I first saw her face four years ago struck my body. She took one look at me, and her eyes began to gloss over. Her skin turned pale and goose bumps formed over her arms. Slowly, two quivering hands covered her wide-opened mouth. Amy's whole body began to slowly shake. Harrison took his pen, pointing at me, and then at Amy. Looking back and forth between us, his eyes locked onto mine, crossing his arms.

"I told myself I'd find you, babe."

A Crash into Reality

As morning approaches, the sun beams in through a hole in the curtains. The light shines on me and I glare at him. A cold breeze of the window that is left open combs through his hair. Playing his monotone alarm, I shake the bed to try and wake him. Tossing around in bed, he flips me off the bed and buries himself in the covers. He grunts as he tries to shut me up. With the swing of one hand and eyes still closed, he tries to pick me off the ground. Touching me with hands as cold a ice, I freeze up and trip over my words. I light up with anticipation as he gets up and starts his day. As he opens his eyes and looks at me, I can see his sharp blue eyes contact as the light hits them.

Every night it's the same. The window is left open to let out the smoke of his "new style cooking" that never ends well. A set bedtime is never in his vocabulary. He writes down in his reminders and notes that he needs to get more sleep, but dismisses it to watch an episode of Hoarders then proceeds to clean the entire place. A sleep deprived cleaning session ends with his bloodshot eyes looking up International House Hunters and googling "Does a hut on an island come with wifi?" Like clockwork, he always wakes up late then scrambles around when he realizes what time it is.

If only he didn't ignore me and snooze off, he wouldn't have to rush to work.

He puts me on the edge of the bed and lets his body swing to the side letting his feet drop to the rustic hardwood floors. The floorboards creak with each step he takes into the other room to get ready; distracting him from me as I shout out his daily schedule. In one hand he brushes his not so pearly whites and in the other, he holds me at eye level, as he begins reading events that happened over night.

His eyes drift off my face, wandering around the room looking all over. A tight grip surprises me, and he takes a deep. The look he is giving in the mirror is different, it looks lost, or he is just dozing off again. Drool hanging off of his lip he spits out the toothpaste and walks out of the bathroom. Leaving the bathroom, he places me back on the sink, hitting the play button before he walks out. Instantly, I begin playing Rebecca Black's Friday song as I hear from the other room his muffled voice singing along. Just as the song is about to end, he comes back in and hits the pause button mumbling "Thank God it's Friday." An overwhelming sense of tension takes over as we walk out of the bathroom and to his closet, where ties begin being thrown on the ground. In the distance I can over hear his voice echoing throughout the closet. A loud thump is followed by him shouting about the heat in the room. The temperature in the room is draining me out, wanting me to go back to bed and restart the day. The music stops and I know he'll get mad if something goes wrong again. Skipping over me, he picks ups everything off his floor. Last week he Googled how to tell if you have OCD; it ended with him on the floor of his closet crying while reading a butchered article on WebMD. A switch goes off and he is suddenly glued to me. The tight grip of his fingers around me, ensure me of his full attention. A smile is lifted onto his face when he looks at me. Though I love being the center of him, it gets exhausting sometimes. I notice in conversations when he is supposed to be listening to someone, he only pays attention to me. I notice sometimes when he is out with others, he only will talk to me, have me out on a podium, face shoved against mine. His hair even gets caught on me when he holds me close. Once I overheard a conversation with his boss, who didn't know I was listening of course, that I consume his everyday life. Whether this is true or not I was humbled by the defense against me that he stood up for me and protected me. Wherever he goes, I go. We have a connection-he is me and I am him.

The clock strikes 8:30, and his first meeting is in a half hour. He starts asking me all sorts of questions; the usual traffic, commute to work, and the news again. At the top of my voice I yell to him, the volume scratches his ears.

The traffic on the highway will take about twenty minutes to get to work.

Not taking into account parking and other incidentals. I can see him getting stressed. He emerges from the closet with two different colored socks on and a plaid tie that clashes his striped suit. Sweat beading down the chin, he runs into the kitchen. I plop into the kitchen chair and almost slip through the cracks on the seat. Preoccupied with getting ready, he neglects to notice me. An absence of attention only leads to me to more frustration. In the corner I can see him ripping open the fridge, his eyes widen as the expired milk and rotten plum buried back into the fridge won't cut it. Opening Uber Eats I shout to him, exclaiming that he can just have me order him food.

The clouds crowd the sun, but let a little bit of light shine through the frosted windows right onto me. The warmth makes me feel special again, like someone is paying attention to me again. The sun slowly fades away, casting a grey cloud in the room. He makes his way out of the kitchen grabbing his wallet and his briefcase. Running around causing commotion, he forgets me in his path. The door shuts and shakes the whole house. It's common, it happens. He forgets me sometimes. Running around for other things, usually I'm right by his side. We all forget sometimes. Every morning it's something. Two times, I have been left behind. Each time I meet back up with him he greets me as if we have never seen each other.

Faint footsteps get louder and the door swings wide open. One shoe off, the other in hand, he limps towards me and we head for the car.

The sky is grey, and in the distance, a small group of snowflakes trickling down. A few flurries hit my face and melt immediately. He wipes them off, making sure not a drop of water is on me. Scrambling through his pockets, he begins to look for his keys. Dropping everything to go look for them, he makes me stay outside. The snowflakes building up into my face, but the heat of his touch still on me makes them melt away. A bead a sweat trickles down his forehead and falls onto me. Running out of the house, keys clanking together, he wipes off the sweat and snow but only manages to smudge it around. His hands shake as he puts me on the seat and starts the car.

The windshield wipers creak as they glide over the un-thawed ice on the glass, interrupting the heater screeching over his terrible music choice. I can't stand the headache he calls music anymore, switching off his handcrafted playlist.

"Hey, it was just getting good, c'mon don't just shut off," He says to me as his eyes widen.

I don't feel that warm sensation when he holds me. I scramble to keep a thought as he shakes and nudges me to turn the music back on. I give up on a grudge and play his somewhat undiscovered playlist. Looking down at me, he tries to make a call, shouting at me as if his music was better than the sound of his voice. Tuning out of his conversation with his friend, I over hear them talking about the weather. I can't see through the window, but I do know that there is a 97% chance of more snow later in the day. He starts to talk to me while still talking to his friend. I barely listen as he shouts to his friend about how the tires keep slipping over the packed snow on the roads. His head starts to turn slowly to the right, the words coming out of his mouth sound like slow motion, The brakes squeal as the car slows down to a halt. He starts to whisper to his friend about how a car is flipped and another is wrapped around a tree. In a soft, yet serious tone, he describes the emergency flares melting away the snowflakes drifting in the wind, the people standing on the corner of the street shaking in the cold, and the ambulances lights going off in the snowy fog lighting up the street. His hands grip the wheel tightly. The only thing with more pale than the glowing snow reflecting from the sun is his face.

The guard hesitated as he let the gate up, and let us through. The lights lit up the car like someone was flicking a light switch on and off; making me even dizzier than before. He began to scramble for his things, one by one; picking me up first then the wallet, keys and brief-case. I can feel his heart beating in the palm of his hand.

I usually don't spend most of the day right by his side. He's often in meetings or preoccupied in meaningless conversations about who won the game the previous night. I don't think about it too much when he doesn't look at me every other minute. It worries me when he is alone and doesn't check on me, my head glitches and I spaz out when his touch doesn't warm me. When I become cold from the loss of touch my emotions go haywire and I shut down.

He tosses me to the side of his desk and grabs a cup of coffee. It's been hours since he's been in here. He came in once and pulled files out of the drawer, even put one folder on me and didn't push it off.

The door creeks open, he frantically walks over to me. His touch quickly recharges me. Gathering up his coat and other personal items we head for the door. Throwing his stuff into the back, I am placed in the passenger seat. The lights in the car garage, flicker on and off. The orange glow of the lights flash into the car as he drives. He keeps checking me for something. I don't understand how he can multitask like this; he can barely hold me without dropping me.

I glare at him as he gets a call from Lucy. She captivates his attention without giving him a headache. He never looks at me whenever we are all together. I tried making noises to get him to look at me, I even buzz with excitement to get him to pay attention to me. I overheat with emotions. I shut down, and drop his call. Letting go of me, I slip out of his hands and sink into the seat between the cushions. His eyes drift off the road. With one hand on the wheel he looks down on the ground to pick me up. I start to turn on when as his fingers barely grasp me. His eyes widen and begin to grow pale, like he did before. It's different this time; I can barely see anything, but I see the window begin to shatter. His face freezes, the once crisp blue eyes fade into a grey grim look. He squeezes me tightly like never before.

I feel a faint overwhelming rush of excitement. Has he finally realized how important I am to him? He lets go of me and I toss and turn like that one time he accidently left me in the wash room. This time clothes aren't being tossed around with suds everywhere, it's just us in the car. My intentions are good; I never meant to hurt anyone. I am shattered.

The Senatorial Predicament

It was a Tuesday morning in Frankfort, Kentucky. I walked out the front door and the heat hit me like a brick wall, walking to my car I admired my beautiful lawn; the dew on the grass glistened as the door to my Cadillac swung open. Already late to work, I found myself sweating through my light blue polo dress shirt, a daily occasion. As I sat down in the leather seat, it scorched me. Reaching down to get my phone from my briefcase, I realized I'd left it inside. Through the sweat and aggravation, I went storming back into the house and my wife was standing in the hallway next to coat rack. With rage in my eye, we made eye contact.

"Forgetting something, dear?" she chuckled with a smile on her face.

"Thank you," I replied softly, diffusing my rage for the morning. I poured a cup of coffee and walked out the front door, I stepped out onto the walkway and my shoes sounded like a horse on pavement until I stepped into my car, turning on 89.7 AM on the radio as I do everyday.

"Election Day only three short months away!" the light voice said. " The polls are looking very good for Mr. Kirkman so far." I rolled my eyes because I was hearing that for the tenth straight day now.

"Today we have a special program where we take callers from all over Kentucky, Go ahead Amy you're on air," the soft voice said swiftly.

"Hi, I just wanna say I hate Mr. Kirkman- if he wins this election, I'm moving far away from Kentucky!" I quickly turned off the radio, I had never heard anything like that on the radio until now.

As I continued driving to my office, I saw all the election signs on each house's front lawn, many prominently displaying my name in bold, red letters. It was becoming too real that my bid for senator of Kentucky was inching closer and closer to the decisive moment. Pulling up to my office, my staff was waiting at the door, like clockwork, to greet me with what laid ahead of us for the day.

"Morning Mr. Kirkman!" Glen, the new intern shouted.

He was always too chipper in the morning- a young boy who was hoping to one day become a senator himself, always rearing at the bit to do anything, but somehow thought that involved having a smile plastered on his face. He was a very smart kid, but from my background, I believe he won't make it a day in the world of politics. The kid's just too nice, he will be taken advantage of from day one. Politics isn't an easy career for someone with paper-thin skin.

"Aye, Mr. Kirkman, how's it going!" asked Chris, the janitor.

"Hi Chris, great to see you." I loved the work this man has done, he may have such a small job here, but he does it right and with a smile on his.

"Good morning, Mr. Kirkman," my assistant, Carol, said with a huge smile on her face.

"Morning Carol, did you get those papers signed for me?" I said.

I sat down at my desk and logged into my computer while looking at the newspaper. The headline, in all capital letters, read, *NEW YORK LAWYER CAPTURES HISTORIC CASE.* Underneath it sat a picture of my eldest son, Michael, in the courtroom. As I read on about the case, my phone rang . It was my other son, Tommy.

"Hey Tommy, what's up buddy?" I said taking another sip of coffee.

"Dad did you see the newspaper- crazy, right?" he said. I could hear his students in the background.

"Yeah, I actually just read it, I'm so excited for him," I explained as I heard a knock on my door, my campaign manager came strolling in.

"Sorry Tom; gotta go," I said as I hung up.

"Only a couple more months until you are the new senator of Kentucky, boss!" he explained with a smile as big as his ego.

"Can't wait, Mark," I said calmly as I took another sip of coffee.

"Come on, sir, you have a press conference waiting outside the office," Mark said to me handing me the agenda for the day.

On my way home from the office, all I could think about was the papers I still had piled up on my desk and all the phone calls I had taken through the day. All this work was catching up to me. My eyes glanced up at the stop light and I slammed on my breaks almost going straight through a red light. As the tires screeched and the smoke rose, the thought of maybe I'm too old for this shot through my head, maybe I'm not ready for this. Then I thought of my wife, she always knew how to make me feel happy, we have been married for 34 years and she was my best friend. I remember laying my eyes on her for the first time- I was in law school and she was an art major. Walking to class I noticed her and I fell in love instantly. There seemed to be 10,000 butterflies in my stomach, and my heart beat faster than I knew it could. Even after the most stressful of days, I knew I had her smile to come home to. I got out of my car and smelled tonight's dinner of baked chicken and mashed potatoes through the screen in the windows

"Hi sweetie," I yelled as I walked through the door, while being tackled by our dog, Buck. She came over and gave me a kiss and whispered

"Sit down for dinner before it gets cold," As I sat down for dinner, she asked, "How was your day?"

"It was very stressful, and I almost died on the way home," I chuckled.

"Aw I'm sorry to hear that, It will all be over soon," she explained.

"Not soon enough!" I said eating another piece of meatloaf.

"Oh by the way, I have a doctor's appointment next Monday," she explained.

I looked at her with a confused look on my face.

"Yah know, the appointment I go to every year?" she said with a hint of sarcasm.

"Oh that's right! Good, thanks for letting me know, honey. I assume everything is going to be alright correct?"

"Let's hope so!" She chuckled

In my mind I knew it scared her that she was going to the doctors but she seemed content and I didn't want to make her more nervous than she already was. So I needed to change the subject.

"This chicken is great, dear," I bragged, shoveling another forkful of mashed potatoes in my mouth.

She loved when I complimented her cooking it made her feel warm inside and I loved seeing her slight smile peek out of her face like the morning sun peeking out of the horizon. That was the same smile she had when I told her I was running for senator too- that was such a great day. This smile I loved so much because when she uses it I know she is proud of me and will stick with me through thick and thin, and that's what this election has been.

"Don't forget- Michael and Tommy are coming over tomorrow night for dinner," she reminded me, picking up the plate off the table.

"I totally forgot about that" Now annoyed that I would have to cancel my meeting with the Mayor of Louisville which was going to be talking about him endorsing me within the next few weeks if the rally is successful. "I guess I can clear my schedule."

◉ ◉

I woke up and looked at my calendar for the day. *LOUISVILLE RALLY* was circled in red on my calendar and underneath that read *Mary*. Why was this in capital letters? I thought in my head.

"Oh that's right-her doctor's appointment," I whispered to myself.

Today was a huge day, my opponent was from Louisville and I knew I had to get all the votes from this city in order to win the election. I got in my Cadillac as I did every morning seeing the same campaign signs each and every day, listening to the same backlash I hear about me. I got to my office and it was a mess. Papers flying, staff members yelling, and phones ringing in many directions, like something out of a movie. Everyone knew it was a huge day for our campaign, all of us didn't have to be at the rally until two. I had no clue why everyone was rushing and making things worse. After going over my speech for the tenth time. I took time to call my wife.

"Hi, are you ready for your appointment?" I said through the phone, scanning through my speech.

"Of course dear, don't worry about me I'll be fine. Good luck at your rally, wish I could have been there for you, but I have this stupid appointment. I know how much this speech means to you I'm really sorry, god I wish I could be there.

"It's okay. Please don't beat yourself up about this; there will be plenty more."

"Okay, you're the best. Have an amazing speech dear."

"Thank you, I'll talk to you later I love you,"

"Love you, too," she said as she hung up the phone.

Mark tapped on the window to my office and gave me the motion to start heading out as he pointed to his solid gold watch. I gathered my things and headed out for one of the most important speeches of my life.

The crowd of 7,000 erupted as Mark came and hugged me, as I ended my speech. Cheers behind the stage rang through my ears as all my staff came to congratulate me on what they called an amazing speech. I took a minute to check my phone and saw I had three missed calls from my wife. A feeling of fear ran through my spine like a bad chill. A million thoughts went through my head, maybe she wasn't okay. I was very busy but I would do anything for Mary so I needed to call her. As I went to call her, Mark came in the room and was pulling me to go take pictures with supporters for the news, so I took another look at my phone. Shaking my head, my finger taped the decline button.

Later, I invited my staff out to dinner to thank them for doing a great job so far. We sat down at a huge table in the middle of the dining room.

"Everything is on me tonight!" I shouted out, hearing cheers from across the table. We ordered our first round of drinks, everyone except for Glen got a cocktail. After the appetizers came out and two beers deeper I was having a conversations with Mark and my phone rang again. It was Mary. I looked at it and clicked on the call later button and continued talking to Mark about where the rest of the campaign was going to go from this point. After I enjoyed a nice prime rib Mark pulled me aside.

"Sir, look over there," he said pointing towards the coat rack. "That's

Robert Conway, I spoke to his company about a big endorsement and he said it could come with a lot of cash for the campaign."

"Let's go talk to him, and see if he is still interested."

I took two steps towards the coat rack and my phone began to vibrate in my pocket.

"Mr. Conway! Great to see you, this is Mr. Kirkman," Mark said, introducing me to him.

I looked at my phone and had to silence it once again. Two calls from Mary and it we weren't even at dessert yet. But I couldn't pass up this opportunity and Mary could wait till I got home. She would surely understand I was busy. 450 dollars later it was time to go home and see Mary

After dinner I drove home listening to the radio.

"Mr. Kirkman had an amazing speech today in Louisville, lifting his polls up past his opponent," said the man on the radio.

I smiled, as my car turned into the driveway. Opening the door and walking inside, Buck was there, as always, to greet me. Jumping up on, he put his paws on my chest as he began to lick my face, his sign that he'd missed me that day. The sentiment was shared by Michael and Tommy, both standing in the door, smiling back at me.

"Dad! Long time no see!" Michael shouted out, wrapping his arms around me.

"Hey Dad," Tommy chimed in, kneeling down to pet Buck .

I went into the kitchen and grabbed a water bottle from the fridge.

"Dad, we missed you at the marathon last week," Michael said.

I took a second before answering, thinking about how I had always been at their running events. A part of me broke off hearing those words come from Michael's mouth. But I was just too busy.

"That was last week?" I asked. "I thought it was next week, how did it go?"

"It was good, I came in seventh and Tom came in tenth," he explained.

"Yeah I was dying near the end," Tom chuckled.

"That's great boys, I wish I could have been there for the both of you but you gotta understand how busy I am lately with the election so close,"

"It's alright we totally understand, our dad is gonna be the Senator of Kentucky, there's no better reward than that," Tom said. Mary came walking in and sat down on the couch. I could tell by her slow dragged out walk something was wrong.

She looked at me with red swollen eyes. I knew something was wrong as soon as she turned her head towards. Walking over to her, the couch made a squeaking noise as I sat down. Grabbing her cold hands, I asked what was wrong. Looking at me, a tear fell down her cheek.

"They found." She stopped choking back tears. Silence filled the room. " They found a lump on my right breast." The words didn't process through my brain and I stood there speechless. Michael and Tommy sat in shock, both lowering their heads in silence. A tear rolled down my face as I hugged her tight. The boys got up and walked towards us and sat down on the couch. Hearing this was a big punch in the gut. The amount of stress our whole family has been through up to this point, and now this. "Why me:, why Mary?" I said to myself. She didn't deserve this. None of us did. My eyes swelled soon followed by tears coming down like a slight drizzle on a cold winter day. I could hear the boys sniffling in the background.

"Everything is going to be okay Mary."

"You look beautiful," I said, unplugging my phone from the charger.

Mary was now on month two of treatment and pills. She looked stunning in her blonde wig, you couldn't even tell it was one. She smiled at me fixing the little hairs that had been sticking out. As she walked into the bathroom my phone rang and it was from an unknown number.

"Hello?" I answered.

"Hi Mr. Kirkman, this is Tory from the Health Daily for Women. I had just had a couple questions concerning you cutting our budget here in Kentucky if you do get elected as Senator."

"Oh hello, right now is really not a good time," I said looking through my dress shirts.

"Mr. Kirkman do you know that our group gives medication to nearly half or the state of Kentucky?" she said promptly.

"Yes, I know but Tory this isn't a good time."

"Mr. Kirkman I don't care, I need answers from you. What you're doing to us is *not okay!*" she finished yelling.

"Tory there's nothing I can do!"

"Mr. Kirkman, you have no idea what you're doing." she said then abruptly hung up the phone.

My heart sank. I knew what I was doing was wrong. But it was just too much money spent over past years, but the people don't see that. But now that Mary is a part of this group it hit me. This is strictly a business decision, and no one is seeing this from my point of view.

I pulled up my tie and headed out the door, not saying goodbye to Mary knowing how guilty I felt about this whole situation. On my way to work I passed by the Women's Health Center I couldn't even look at it. All the wrong things I was thinking in my head were eating away at me.

❧   ❧

I woke up to the alarm buzzing and by accident I hit the radio button instead of snooze. The past month has been from hell. Mary has had many doctor appointments and is doing very well. I still have the Health group up my ass but I'm doing everything I can to work it out.

"Two day until the election!" said the radio man as I smashed my hand down on the alarm clock. I didn't want to hear it. It was all going too fast. Mary wasn't feeling well and I had reporters up my ass and I hadn't slept in months. My stress levels were off the roof. Still the thought of hiding something from Mary killed me everyday.

"Let's go, hun." I said to Mary as she was getting ready. We got into my car and drove to the diner . As I got out of the car, reporters rushed me as 1000 voices hit me like a brick wall. I helped Mary out of the car.

"Mr. Kirkman, how can you justify cutting the budget on the women's health group when your very own wife is struggling with some of the things they treat?" a reporter shoved his recorder near my face, eyes wide, hoping for something that he could plaster on the front page of tomorrow's paper.

"How is your wife knowing you cut the budget on the women's health group?" a reporter said.

My heart sank. Mary looked at me and she had that disappointed look on her face. She just kept walking without me.

No one had known about this until it became plastered all over the Channel 6 News. *Candidate Kirkman plans to cut Women's Health Group budget* ran across the screen over and over again, making me feel worse and worse.

"For those of you who don't know Mr. Kirkman plans on cutting the budget that controls the Women's Health Group here in Kentucky. This budget funds all women's medication and needs based on Medical issues to ensure everyone has an equal chance of a healthy lifestyle." said the reporter standing outside the group's headquarters. Hearing this I sat in my recliner chair going over my platform. Mary was in the kitchen watching Wheel of Fortune, but something was different tonight. She wasn't her regular self, screaming the words she knew to the tv screen. Tonight it was silent. I continued to avoid her, dinner was silent, until the silence broke. While cleaning she took my plate and smashed it into sink. The glass shattered everywhere. I knew she was frustrated now. We got into the bedroom for bed, I noticed my clothes thrown all over my closet with no hangers in sight.. As I took a step towards my closet to fix this mess and hang up my clothes Mary stepped in front of me.

"You have to do something about this." she said in a stern voice.

"Mary I can't tear apart my platform this late in the election." I said

She looked at me like she was about to say something, she stopped and turned the light off. "End of conversation I guess" I said to myself.

Walking into the headquarters the next day, Mary was still in the forefront of my mind. The words from our conversation continued to play over in my head, as if looping on a broken record, each time making me feel more and more guilty for what I was proposing. Each time it'd play over in my head, I became a bit more confused- was I angry with her, or angry with myself? These thoughts came to a grinding halt as Mark walked over to me.

"I think you need a press conference explaining how Mary is battling breast cancer. It's the only way to gain the votes we need back." he said. No one had know about this. We wanted to keep it between our staff only. It had to be done.

Later that day I got up in front of tons of people in downtown Frankfurt.

"Good Afternoon. I wanted to say that I will not be cutting the budget on the Women's Health Group." Claps slowly started to get louder. " I have something else that has affected my decision. My wife, Mary, has been battling breast cancer for two months now. She is my everything and I would never do anything to hurt her." The crowd erupted with claps. "So I hope all of you watching at home understand and forgive me for my wrong decision, but no one's perfect and I hope I can get your vote tomorrow in the election." The crowd rose in astonishment, all I could hear is the roaring of the crowd clapping.

"Final polls close in 10 minutes" said the tv host on Fox news. The race was tight and it was too close to call in Kentucky. I was standing next to my sons and Mary watching the television like a child. My staff all on their feet in our room behind the stage were worried. The thought kept going through my head, Did I do enough? Was I going to pull this off? Was this more important than taking care of Mary? Will it pay off? My mind was going in thousands of directions. I stopped overthinking as the tv said,

"The final results are in….." The entire room went silent. My heart was beating faster than a sports car on an open highway.

"The winner of the Senate race in Kentucky is Dan Kirkman."

New Land, New Love

Another day living with my parents is another day I waste," Joseph murmured as he stared at the Andes Mountains in the far distance. Sitting on the front porch was one of his favorite things to do-it was a way for him to relax and think about the perfect future- a steady paying job, a welcoming neighborhood, and a one bedroom apartment designed for a bachelor.

The grating noise of pebbles being chucked around informed Joseph that the paper bay was coming down the road. The newspaper flew into the sky and landed a couple feet away. Prying himself from the chair, Joseph sighed vehemently, and begrudgingly picked up the pile of papers as he thought about the vile news he was about to read. Over a decade ago, Joseph's home country fought with the United States and the rest of the Allies. Battle horses were transported from the southern hemisphere to the northern hemisphere, where all the Allies resided. Argentina was threatened to be punished after providing main transportation for the troops. All that was on his mind was the fun the United States and France must have had riding their horses throughout different areas of the world. The only thing that he didn't understand was the economy: it was plummeting rapidly and it seemed to set him ablaze. The words stared at him with their bolded shapes; he forced his eyes to read beyond the title, *"Shocking News: Economy Crashing In World's Superhouse"*. He heard about this issue only a few months before, but it seemed like everyday the situation got worse. Enraged by this unsettling news, Joseph balled up the newspaper fervently, and while his mind wandered with thoughts of the future, he stood. He stood because in that moment, that was all he was capable of.

"San Juan is not the place for me. I am an adventurous young man who wants to start my own life some place far away from here. Doesn't anybody get it?" he abruptly exclaimed as he launched the paper into the garbage can with full strength. "My family is hanging by a thread, and once it snaps, we will all fall into a financial pit hole that would be impossible to escape." Joseph didn't want to hear about other people's depressing lives; his was stodgy enough.

Being in the presence of pessimism only perpetuated Joseph's unhappiness. His thoughts of his future caused him to wander into the city of San Juan, only about a half of mile away from his house, which resided on the border of the area. Walking next to the San Juan River somehow calmed his nerves and helped his mind flow. He couldn't help but continue to think about his family whenever he'd make the trip by the river. It was the only place where they would seem like a family, where his father wouldn't worry about finances, where his mother wouldn't be doing backbreaking house work, and where his siblings would let their imaginations wander. As he walked down the river, he came upon a sight that severely took his breath away. Multitudes of people standing around with suitcases and packages, and young children threw rocks into the ocean, chasing each other in circles. Officials collecting tickets and payments for the trip surrounded a boat that was close to departure. He knew what this could mean.

Joseph's thoughts ran faster than his feet; as his mind raced, he wondered where the boat was going. His mind picked up a metronomical pace and kept time with his feet. He whizzed by, "Opportunity", "new life", "employment", "stability"... he gasped out the words inaudibly as he raced home. Almost as fast as his mind, he tapped a man close by him, grabbing his attention.

"Excuse me, sir, but where is this going?" He stared at the man, waiting for an answer.

"All these people are going to the greatest country in the world, the United States of America!", the man grinned a toothless grin, a grin that read of only purity, pure joy, almost innocence.

A neatly manicured green lawn. A two-story Victorian era home.

Neatly pleated red shutters. A driveway. But above all, what did Joseph really want? He wanted normalcy. He wanted assimilation. He wanted excitement and a fresh start. He wanted America. Was this selfish? Perhaps. He let his mind indulge in the future; he blocked out those thoughts of fear, those thoughts of rejection. Maybe America would chew him up and spit him back out.

But he was still determined to try.

"Mom! Dad!" Joseph hollered, as he threw open the front screen door of his house. His brow covered in sweat from his long walk home, he seemed almost out of breath as he greeted his parents.

"Si, Joseph? Que pasa?" his mother asked with concern, her face filled with distraught as she quickly put down her cutting knife as she stopped preparing dinner.

He managed to choke down his excitement long enough to reply with a delicate and persuasive tone, "Nothing is wrong, Mom." He took a deep breath. "I just got back from the docks on the river. So many people were there, all trying to leave for America." His father, straggling in from his afternoon *siesta*, scuffed a guttural moan. Joseph hated how his father condemned America and her hardworking discipline. How could he judge her if he never mustered up the courage to visit? Joseph continued bravely, already anticipating the worst. " How great would it be for us to join them?"

Silence echoed throughout the room for what seemed like eternity, until it was finally broken by the sound of the boat's horn in the distance. Joseph's father met Joseph's opportunistic eyes. "Dad, how incredible would it be if we could get out of here? You can finally get a good job," he looked up at his father with eyes full of yearning.

His parents glanced at each other before they locked their wandering eyes back to Joseph.

"Honey, we know how determined you are to be successful. But how could we get on without you here?" His mother's voice cracked as her eyes fell from Joseph's gaze to the floor. Joseph could feel his dream shatter with each word.

"With my job not paying enough for us to get by, it is important that you contribute to support of our family. You need a job here, one that will help us all," his father demanded now getting defensive.

Joseph's heart sank to his stomach. How could he leave his family? Dragging his feet across the chipped, oak wood floor, Joseph pulled himself up the stairs and plopped his sluggish body on his bed. Guilt and disappointment flooded into his heart knowing that there was no way out of the city. Watching the sun disappear behind the mountains as the shadows begun run rampant across the fields, Joseph surrendered himself to his permanent life in Argentina.

Joseph awoke abruptly to his father angrily mowing the lawn. If there was one thing he learned about his father, it was that he took out his passive aggressive nature on the house, which wasn't always a bad thing. After being disturbed by the constant roaring of the lawn mower, Joseph dragged himself out of bed and lingered down the stairs, just barely crawling into the kitchen.

"What would you like for breakfast?" Joseph's mother asked while inching a plate of scrambled eggs and ketchup in his direction, hoping he will give into his favorite breakfast.

"Nothing," mumbled Joseph as he made his way from the stairs to his favorite spot in the living room, right in the corner where nobody disturbed him.

His mother's enthusiasm was drained out of her face. Strolling into the kitchen, his father followed the smell of the eggs. He noticed the disappointment etched into his wife's upper brow. He pondered this, and consequently called his son into the kitchen. Slouched in a baggy sweatshirt, Joseph shuffled across the kitchen floor, the disappointment twinkling sadly in his eyes.

"Joseph..." he trailed off, trying to find the right words to say.

His mother interrupted before he could collect his thoughts and continued, "Joseph, as painful as it is for us to let you or any of your siblings go, we want you to go to the United States. You are right, it would be great for you to join them and get yourself out there.

While standing in shock, Joseph's eyes widened and a look of confusion spread across his face.

"Don't second guess yourself. It's better that you move on, don't worry about the rest of us. Your father and I will take care of the house and the family, that's our job not yours," his mother added, trying to fight back the tears.

The voyage seemed to go on for centuries. At this rate, he would die before he even got there. The loud, bothersome ride that dictated the emotions of all on board seemed to primarily affect women, children, and the elderly. They were exempt from standing like the men; some of the men seemed to get rowdy and uncomfortable. During the trip, Joseph felt seasick every day for a month. The waves rocked his stomach back and forth disturbing any meal he would try to eat. All the movement made it look like the world had no stability. Nights in the overflowing quarters only made his nausea worse, especially when he tripped over people walking to the small-scale bathroom. When he felt an anxiety attack coming on, Joseph forced himself to think of good things: elegant restaurants, comfortable beds, and a bedroom that had an attached bathroom for situations like this.

"You know what I heard? These lousy Americans aren't accepting any people from Asia. They are stuck in their countries, and I don't understand why they can't come here," stated a father of three young children.

Joseph quickly chimed in with concern, "It's not only the Asians, but the Irish as well. Thousands are entering the country looking for jobs and a better future. We're lucky for the fact that we are allowed to come to this country. What's going to be challenging is finding a job. I read in the newspaper that people are getting laid off because of banks failing and a smaller demand for products. Since the war, companies haven't been selling nearly as many products as they did during the war so they let their employees go. I pray that everyone here is able to start their new life on the right foot." Joseph breathed. How long did that take him? He reasoned that the excitement was settling in.

Joseph made his way through lower Manhattan, after he departed from the southern harbor, not too far from Wall Street. Hundreds of men and women were gathered in front of buildings that housed the economy for not only the city, but the whole country. Many obtained signs reading *"ON STRIKE"* and *"APPALLED BY WALL STREET!"* With all the commotion everywhere, Joseph connected the pieces and figured that most of the banks resided on Wall Street, and they were failing. People ranting in front of the towers didn't help, all it did was cause trouble. The amount of disrespect that ran throughout the streets alarmed Joseph. Citizens from all ages were blocking roads and fighting police officers who were trying to keep order in the area.

"Excuse me, sir. Don't just stand there and stare at us, grab a sign and start shouting," proclaimed a young lady, her face scrunched as her eyes narrowed, staring at me. Her skirt was covered in stains and her shoes weren't any better; Joseph could see small holes forming in them.

Joseph stared at her as if she had three heads and failed to respond. The foreign words falling out of her mouth were difficult for him to comprehend, all he knew was he didn't want to participate in the protest. Since he had just stepped foot in the country, he didn't want to start any trouble. While shaking his head, Joseph left before the police came to break up the protesting and riots. As his travelling lead him further into continued the foreign country, he noticed how lively the city was despite of The Great Depression. Street bands were performing jazz in the busiest areas of New York City. Their music filled the air with anticipation and hope as the sweet sound of medic chords danced into the ears of plenty, causing them to get lost in the world of music instead of finances. Children played in the gutters, while their mothers complained of how much their husbands had to work just for them to purchase food at a market. New York City reminded Joseph of home. The buildings towered, blocking out the sun that would scorch the city around noon. Attractive avenues and busy streets were just like the ones in San Juan, except they were packed with double the amount of people. Walking on the sidewalk next to Central Park gave Joseph the soothing feeling he would get when walking next to the San Juan River. Noticing large groups of people made him think of his family back home. Each of his siblings had their own distinctive personality and features, yet they all belonged to one family. The members of this community originated from all over the world, yet they now belonged to New York City. The only significant difference was that no one spoke Spanish. The unfamiliar words flowed into Joseph's ears when people opened their mouths.

Almost no one spoke his language, but staying positive was key for his only other issue was finding a job. "I'm going to have to learn English, no other way around it."

Searching the streets for a job brought nothing but bad luck to Joseph. Men from all ages crowded around Pierce and Sherman Agencies desperately searching for work; he was losing hope. Kicking the dirt that lay beneath the crumpled newspapers and old candy wrappers, Joseph started to become very anxious.

"How is a 20 year old man with only $20 suppose to obtain a comfortable life?!" Joseph exclaimed to no one in particular, clenching his jaw and holding back emotions, even though all he wanted to do was scream. Back in Argentina, $20 was enough to buy groceries for the next month. Coming into this country, Joseph assumed it would be enough to at least be able to put a down payment on an apartment or have a stable food supply. But since he arrived during the worst part of The Great Depression, $20 could only get him a couple of meals at a local restaurant. All he saw was "CLOSED" and "NOT HIRING" signs on store doors. After hours of desperately searching, Joseph stumbled upon an open store and thrust the door open. A man near the cash register stared as he approached him. He stood at an intimidating tall height, had neatly combed blonde hair, and a rounded face. Despite his size, he seemed inviting and smiled at Joseph making him feel welcomed.

"Hello, sir. What can I get you today? We have our early bird special: $8.50 for a breakfast of ham, bacon, eggs, applesauce, and a slice of toast with any drink you choose."

Staring at the man for a few seconds while trying to catch his breath, Joseph handed him a newspaper with "job" circled. It was too difficult for to explain that he needed to start working.

The man glanced at the sign and paused, "I am looking for a dishwasher, would you be interested? I don't think it's too difficult to grasp."

Focusing hard on the words escaping the man's mouth, Joseph tried to make out familiar sounds of the English language. The only thing he was certain of was the word "job", a word everyone mentioned and familiarized themselves with on the boat. Not thinking twice, Joseph said "yes" and followed the man who introduced himself as Paul to the back of the small restaurant.

The excitement ran through Joseph's body like a million lightning bolts. His new life in America would finally take off. All Paul told him to do was wash the dishes that were collected from the tables. He stood proudly in front of the sink with dozens of melamine plates, cups and bowls covered in leftover ketchup and egg. The silverware made its way to the bottom of the sink, so Joseph didn't feel the need pay too much attention to them. Plates were stacked in columns next to his station ready for the cooks to grab them and go. Even though the work was backbreaking, Joseph wasn't granted any breaks. The pain from standing for an extended period of time crawled up from his lower back to the muscles right at his shoulder blades. After one of the waiters came back into the kitchen, there was a faint grunt that came from the customer tables.

"This is disgusting. I didn't pay good money for my plates to be covered with someone else's leftovers. Do you want my son to eat the scrapings of another's meal?" the man hollered at the waiter who made his way back into the kitchen.

After a few minutes, Paul stormed in angry as someone who stepped in water with socks on. Sweat raced down the sides of his face, deep purple veins popped out of the sides of his neck, and his eyes bulged out of their sockets. The comforting smile Joseph first saw had been erased and forgotten, only to bring in a monster.

"How hard is it to wash dishes?! What is this?!" Paul pointed to a section on a recently cleaned plate. It looked fine to Joseph. He was always used to spots existing on the plates at home because his mother would always tell him to save water. It was never a big deal until now.

"Are you going to wash the plates like you're suppose to? Or are you going to make the name of my restaurant a disgrace?" Paul screamed in his face making spit fly into Joseph's eyes.

"Wash another dish. I want to see if you're doing this right," he asserted while pointing at the sink, "Wash another dish, come on." All the cooks and other maintenance staff workers froze waiting for his next move. Joseph stared at him completely confused. He washed another dish and placed it on the pile although it still had spots of egg yolk.

"You can't even remove the food off of one little plate!" Paul roared while taking the plate and throwing it into the ground, pieces flying everywhere.

"You're fired!" screamed Paul while his eyes locked on Joseph's.

Heart pounding, Joseph stood in shock and his face turned red with embarrassment. He didn't know what Paul was saying. After a full minute of not moving, Paul seemed to realize that Joseph hadn't had a clue as to what he was to do. Grabbing him by the sleeve, Paul forcefully dragged him all the way to entrance.

"Out you idiot!" He shouted while pointing outside. Joseph's heart sank when he realized his first step to a new future disintegrated right before his eyes, he could understand that Paul wanted him gone. He lost all hope in America.

Sleeping on the benches of Central Park during the blazing summer nights and sharing invading shelters with other immigrants made Joseph regret coming to America . He even saw children begging in the streets for food instead of attending school at the local schoolhouse. At one point during the brutal winter, Joseph decided to forfeit all financial rights and move into a tenant house along with countless numbers of immigrants and other low income citizens. The tenements were less than a foot apart from each other which allowed for small amounts of air to flow into the buildings. Luckily, Joseph's small room was on the side that faced the street. Thankfully, his apartment had a small window which let sunlight pour in, and on dark days, the sun seemed to remind him of the light to come, that with every dark night comes a sunny morning. Nature seemed to be on his side...

Things seemed to worsen with each passing week. A week turned into a month, a month turned into 6 months, and by then he was kicked out onto the streets by the landlord. He was left a homeless, hopeless immigrant.

Walking for over 30 blocks to arrive at the overpopulated, homeless shelter, Joseph always ended up at as the day turned to night. People moaned every time they stepped foot into the building. Their scraggly hair and broken clothes gave the area the wrong image. The distinct personalities that lie underneath the skins of people could not bring life to the grey area.

Getting in line for dinner, Joseph stomach gurgled as he began to think about his mother's cooking at home. He noticed the shelter was serving what looked like provoleta, a grilled sandwich that is filled with cheese and herbs. As he collected his tray and utensils, a young woman behind the counter caught his attention with a smile,

"Hello sir, what would you like to eat today?"

Pulling his head up, the two made eye contact. The world around Joseph stopped for a moment as and his heart dropped to his empty stomach. He had never seen anyone so perfect.

"Uhhhh… I'm sorry," he said while pointing at the hamburger, hoping she would realize that is the choice he made.

She smiled and gently placed the food on his plate with her moisturized hand and dusty rose painted nails.

"Thank you ma'am. My name is Joseph, and you are?"

"Mary."

"Nice to meet you, Mary," Joseph said as he made his way to an open seat, trying not to stare.

All through dinner, the thought of Mary's wavy brown hair, perfectly polished face with light pink lipstick, and flowing ankle dress played over and over again in Joseph's mind. His thought encouraged him to rise at the crack of dawn and roam through the whole city seeking for a stable income. Making money to take Mary out was his goal, he wanted to know her more than just a food distributor. The homeless shelter agreed to hire Joseph despite the fact he relied on them for food and housing. While washing dishes of homeless immigrants, Joseph was careful to make sure there weren't any spots on any plates that could risk him losing another job during this economic crisis. Working during the morning and lunchtime was better for Joseph, for he got off of work before Mary came in to volunteer. Each day, he'd look for Mary at the shelter, and jumped into the line she served even if he didn't like the food.

"Hello Joseph. How are you today?" she asked with excitement.

He responded with enthusiasm, "Hi Mary."

"What would you like today?" she stared at him patiently waiting for an answer.

Started to feel tingly, Joseph's breathing became short and his chest tightened, hoping no one noticed that his cheeks were turning a bright red. Joseph took a deep breath, stood up straight, and collected his thoughts before asking his question.

"Mary, would you like to eat dinner with me today?" He swallowed hard and hoped she would say yes. Mary looked surprised, but also serene as if she already knew Joseph was going to ask her.

"I would love to."

As they made their way to a table for two, Joseph finally got the sense that there was hope in the new land.

The Case

Sipping on my morning Italian-roasted coffee and observing Park Ave from a fair distance, I took refuge in the warmth of Regency Hotel. Pay day was in sight and I could feel myself getting more excited by the second. I pulled my sleeve up, gazed down at my watch, and left the coffee bar. The scarf around my neck shielded my cold body from the harsh, Manhattan winter. Glaring up and down the busy streets, I waved my arm in the air as if I were conducting an orchestra and a cab halted to the side of the street immediately. The frostiness of the cab door transcended through my leather gloves, making me shiver as I got inside.

"2 East 55th Street." I exclaimed, watching the driver veer off into traffic in the rush to make miles.

Going from cab to cab lugging my bulky camera around made me grow weary. This was my last job before I was headed towards Cancun, hopefully it wouldn't be too extensive. The faces seemed to all mesh into one, the cases all appeared to be the same, day-in and day-out. This much-needed break coming up alleviated some of the dull stress surrounding the nuisances in my line of work, the thrill of piecing together stories had become sort of stale and repetitive.

My camera bag bounced around behind my shoulder as I got out of the cab hoping to meet and impress a new client. Meeting with William Lasserman, a big-time chief operating officer, would open big doors, financially, for my business. If I got this right, I would be the first man he names to his influential partners whenever they need digging. Sure, it was a one-man business and I was my own boss, but my camera was like my partner in crime. All the gory details I've had the displeasure of witnessing, I've seen through the lens of my camera.

I walked over to the table tucked in the corner near the wall where he waited, pulled out the chair, and took my seat.

"Nathaniel, good to see you. Well, not so good, actually," William greeted me with his head hanging low, rubbing his eyes.

"You're right. You know it's not so good if you're paying me a visit," I responded plainly.

I pulled out my business card and placed it on the table, immediately relieving any ounce of awkwardness. The beginning of all these conversations started the same- all clients usually beat around the bush about what they want at first, but I like being blunt and skipping the "fluff" part of the conversation.

I'll never forget the time I met a crazy client in Central Park. He wore a trench coat, a fedora, and held newspapers in his arms like he was straight out of Mad Men. That nut job planned to stand on opposite sides of water fountain, where he'd knock his umbrella three times on the concrete for me to come talk to him. When I skipped the umbrella part and went straight over to him, I wasn't sure if he was more mad that I was blunt or that he wouldn't get to reenact his favorite old detective novel.

"I ask a fair price for what I do: top of the line: you won't find anyone more discrete and subtle than me. I don't do any less or more of what you ask. That's it," I declared.

William looked over the card, took a sip of coffee, and sighed. I'd seen that look before- in fact, I'd seen it too many times. He was contemplating everything in his mind, *Do I want to admit to myself that my beloved wife would cheat on me? Do I betray her? Or do I save myself?* Those questions had become somewhat of a cliché in my line of work, with a never-ending surplus of untrustworthy and paranoid spouses. Half the time their suspicions are right, but I didn't care for the drama. I brought my camera and did my part of the work. What they then choose to do with the truth is up to them.

"Uhh, yeah. You know what to do. She has yoga every Saturday at 1 P.M., but she's usually gone from 10-3 for no reason, every time I ask, she says she 'hangs out at the yoga place.' I don't even know what yoga place. I just want to start a family, but I need answers before we go that far. My company is also growing and if this ends… we didn't make a pre-nup and it'll look bad to my business partners if my wife cheats on me. I don't know…" William said. It seemed as though he was conceding, already believing the allegations he'd made.

"You have a deal. Meet here around this time next week and I'll show you what's really going on."

I stood up and concluded by wrapping my scarf around my neck, motioning to shake hands, but he stayed seated, with his head hanging low.

Walking away, I pushed through the heavy glass doors. I felt myself grow tired of hunting down cheating spouses, backstabbing business partners, and privileged children betraying their parents. I remember the first time I caught my very first trophy housewife who cheated on her money-hungry husband. Her name, however irrelevant in this case, was Margaret. This was the last time I bothered to remember their names, to me they are all just a "case." I followed this Margaret to pilates, brunches, fundraisers, and the movies.

"12.98 dollars Sir. Just one?" The movie theater employee said.

"Yes, thank you." I responded confidently as I handed over cash. The movies are where it starts to get tough. It was dark and I had to watch, report, and take pictures from a safe distance to protect my cover. Keeping myself at arms-length was difficult considering it was dark and crowded, but I knew I was on the cusp of catching Margaret. I found it odd that Margaret bought herself a ticket for an animated kid's film and neglected to bring her kids. My camera just needed to catch her in the right, or wrong, moments and then hand the proof over to her greedy husband.

This case, Margaret, started off sitting in row B, but went to the bathroom five minutes into the movie. My camera focused in on this case, following her every movement. Through the lens, I saw Margaret return and sit down next to a man in a different row. *What's a man in a suit doing alone in a cartoon movie?* I asked myself. Although I was there, a few rows away watching and analyzing, I was still invisible behind my lens waiting for the proof. Soon enough, I caught Margaret doing some rated R things in a PG-13 cinema.

That was the last time I ever saw that case. *Was she still married? Was it worth it to cheat on her husband in a movie theatre?* These are questions I pondered, but never got any answers to. The honking of New York traffic brought me back to reality, reminding me I was only a block away from my apartment building.

"Thank you sir," I said to the cab driver, stepping out and rushing over to the door.

As I walked into my apartment, I took off my trench coat and hung it in the coat closet. Settling down with my laptop on the couch, I opened a bottle of Montoya Cabernet.

"New York public records directory..." I mumbled to myself as my fingers flew across the keyboard.

I searched "Mia Lasserman" into the directory under criminal records and NY divorce records. The initial checks of each case were so routine and mechanic. I looked her up on Facebook, Twitter, Instagram, and public records. As I started to piece together the case's life, friends, and hobbies I could see the small similarities between her and every other case I've dealt with. The case liked reading romance type books, taking yoga classes, and going on runs. That wasn't the most glamorous or suspenseful part of my job, but it was the getting inside their head and figuring out what made them tick that excited me to follow them and take note. She had joined a Facebook page for a charity event that was raising money for water in Africa that night at seven and as I looked through the comments and pictures, I knew it was the perfect opportunity to scope her out. Clicking through all the males who had RSVP'd "maybe" to the charity event, I kept an eye out for a man my size. With my suit on and my shoes shined, hopefully I can pull off being the ever so elegant "Thomas Penn" tonight. From his Facebook it seemed as though he lead a grandiose life-between dozens of galas he'd posted pictures of to the myriad of cute dog photos he had, he was, for all intents and purposes, a pretty stand up guy. Playing him would be a piece of cake-if only I had a dog.

"Perfect..." I mumbled to myself as I got up to get ready for the event later that night, where I will get to the bottom of the case. The corners of my lips turned up just thinking about the cold margarita I'd have in my hand and the lack of lying couples to investigate.

I pulled my camera from its bag in the cab on my way to the event to check the memory disc and battery, I was ready to capture anything.

"Name?" The lady said with a smile ear-to-ear.

"Thomas Penn," I said with a cunning confidence.

She looked up and down the list, flipping to the next page. She crossed a name over with her pen.

"You're all set-enjoy!" The lady said with a cheery voice.

"Thanks," I responded boldly.

The ballroom was captivating and sparkling, every shard of glass on the chandeliers hung with grace from the ceiling, illuminating the gala event. The tables were designed in a cluster, with a podium at the front. I looked amidst the growing crowd for blonde hair. For some strange reason, I had knots in my stomach. I usually did a much more in-depth profile before planning to observe in person, but the anxiety of going to Cancun and finishing the job had gotten the best of me. My small, black camera bag hung on the chair next to me as I pretended to take a very important phone call, simultaneously scanning the room once again for the case. My phone was practically glued to my ear so that nobody would try to talk to me as I browsed, looking for the woman.

It was her emerald dress that caught my attention at first. The way the long train glided on the floor behind her, following her ceaselessly, making her movements more pronounced. My eyes were drawn to her face because although her makeup was bare and natural-looking, her hair was tucked into a tight updo that caught my attention. The case, with a friend I had recognized from her social media, made their way over to the long banquet table. This case and her sidekick laid out their pricey purses and extravagant coats. When all was said and done, she motioned to her phone and pointed to the exit. I watched like a hawk as she exited the ballroom to seemingly to 'take a call.' This sly exit to a back stairwell raised my suspicion and I was on my toes, ready to follow. I sneakily stood up and walked over to the same stairwell without raising any eyebrows, if the case were going to cheat on her husband I would be right on her heels with my camera.

"Hmm... that's odd." I whispered under my breath as I followed the click-clack noise of heels up the staircase.

There were at least half a dozen elevators in this place- *why use the stairs?* My senses heightened and the peculiarity of the situation had my attention. I rounded each corner delicately turning on my heels and peaking around each staircase discretely.

With the hints of green around the next flight, I carefully and ever so quietly back-treaded to the last flight. I pulled my bag around my waist and diligently took out my camera. The settings were already adjusted to have no sound or flash; I wanted nothing to deter my investigation. My hands positioned the camera around the corner, while the rest of my body lain against the railing. The click-clack of heels paused and I held on to the railing so tight in attempt to keep my balance.

"It's so good to see you..." The case whispered under her breath.

The mysterious departure and whispering had led me to believe William's suspicions were right. I tried to reach my camera out further to be more confident in my shots, but lost my balance in the process of speeding things up. As I tried to regain my balance on the stairwell, my camera tipped just out of my fingers and onto the ground before I could blink. The camera hit the ground with an echoing thud and the pieces flew outwards, leaving the body of my beloved camera broken and disfigured on the ground. Shattered and mangled, the lens laid on the stair facing upwards at me. The fractured glass looked like an eloquent spider web.

"Who's there?!" the case said, scared and confused.

The stiletto heels traveling down reverberated in the stairwell and although I knew I would either have to run or explain myself, my feet stuck to the ground. Surrounded by the crumbled fragments of my camera, I couldn't compose the precise words to say. The case turned around the corner with a bottle of champagne in one hand and the train of her dress gathered in the other hand. Her hair had fallen from that stiff updo into a messy knot while the mystery man at the top of the stairs stood silent.

"I...uh..." I gracefully mumbled. I used to be more confident, even proud of my work. I had never contacted or spoken to a case before-because I simply was not supposed to. Now here I was, jaw-clenched in front of a case with no words and a broken camera.

"It's not what it looks like," she said calmly.

"I don't care what it looks like, I care what it is. I don't need evidence

116

to tell William what I know, but I plan to do my job," I responded matter-of-factly.

"William hasn't been the same since his new job, he works long hours and doesn't love me anymore. I would spend hours away from our house and we didn't even know where I was. Please, don't tell him," She begged.

I knew I should've gathered the remains of my camera, packed my bag, and ran down the stairs. I knew I should've told William everything. I shouldn't have cared about her situation, or why she cheated on her husband. I should've done a lot of other things, but nothing came to mind that could make me move my feet.

"I never knew why cases betrayed the people closest to them, but providing some reason you came up with to justify going behind your husband's back doesn't change anything. All you cases end up the same, so cliche and predictable. I'm telling William and then I am done chasing down people like you," I said.

Anger rose in my voice and even though investigating these Upper East Siders paid my rent, I couldn't bare to take another picture of an affair. I used to wonder why spouses lied, but getting her answers wasn't as satisfying. The words were empty and while she tried to rationalize her actions, nothing about her reasoning made sense. I used to ask myself what would happen after I handed over evidence, but now I don't care. I was looking at this situation through a different lens, a perspective that changes everything.

No matter if I went to Cancun, or stayed in New York, I felt as though this uncertainty would follow me wherever I go, like a shadow on a sunny summer day. The pieces of my camera laid scattered on the ground in ruins. I was unsure if I could ever truly pick up the pieces and investigate a case again.

Opportunity

Tin Pan Alley. The trek on the pitch black streets had become so routine that it was comfortable. The small window of time I had, meant I had to hurry; I ignored the cries from the poor boys who lived on the street corners and the calls from drugstore cowboys who loitered outside every shop. Hurriedly, I stumbled through the dim alleys until I reached the familiar wrought iron gate.

Quickly, I glanced around to make sure I hadn't drawn any attention to myself. From my shoe, I pulled out the rusted key and fumbled around the moss and ivy in an attempt to open the lock. As soon as it popped open, I shoved myself through the opening and slammed it shut behind me. In front of me stood the looming wooden door. Lifting the door knocker, I gave it four quick raps. The sound of jazz music and gleefully drunk conversation from inside halted. The sliding window cracked open as my eyes met those of the man inside. Instantly, his stone glare softened as he recognized my face. I heard the snap of each lock unlatching before the door creaked open. As I slipped inside, I was greeted by the echoing cheers of the friendly crowd.

"Good evening, Kathryn!" they called, their sloppy voices filled with joy. A smile spread on my face as I heard their echoing praise, which dropped off sharply as I began walking towards the bar.

Though the room was packed with people, the clicking sound of my heels rang in the air. The swishing fabric and shimmering beads of my short dress made every head turn my direction as I strut, slowly and assuredly, to meet the bartender. I tucked a strand of my bob behind my ear and leaned on the countertop as I waited.

"Kat," he smiled, taking my hand and kissing the back. "You look dashing, as always," he said, his eyes glancing up and down my frame. I raised my penciled brows and smirked at his gawking expression. Realizing his mistake, he now turned quickly to make my drink. He filled a small glass with the amber liquid and placed it in my open hand, bowing as he stepped back.

As I turned to face the quiet crowd behind me, I saw my regulars: debs trying to forget their problems, dames and their rich husbands, and the old men who bought out entire shelves. I smiled, raising my glass in the air. Breaking the silence, they erupted out in a cheer as they raised their glasses and joined me in a toast. The band resumed its blaring tune while girls in short dresses danced the Charleston with half a cigarette in their mouths. Now that I had my drink, the night had truly begun.

"Hey doll," I heard a low voice from behind me as strong arms wrapped gently around my waist.

"Hello love," I responded warmly, tilting my head back to leave a red lipstick stained kiss on his cheek.

"Great news," he said, pulling out a wad of dough from his pants pocket.

"How much?" I asked eagerly, spinning around to meet his smiling face.

"Guess," he responded with a smirk.

"Fifteen hundred?" I said, already aiming high.

"More," he said, now with a full-fledged grin growing on his face.

"Seventeen hundred?" I questioned in disbelief.

"Twenty-two hundred, doll," he answered proudly, fanning through the thick stack and beaming as he pulled me in for another kiss. As I smashed my glass into Jack's in a celebratory toast, I watched my empire around me flourishing.

I had once been the girl who was bred to believe that she would never become anything more than a wife and mother, just as my own had done. But as I watched my mother cooking mindlessly every night and cleaning early each morning, I soon realized that was not a life for me.

"Kat, come help!" she'd call from the kitchen.

"I don't wanna," I'd cry from my bedroom, hiding under my covers to avoid the task.

"It's not an option!" she'd yell, her voice becoming more shrill as I became more disobedient.

"Dad doesn't have to do any chores," I'd whine. Every day, I'd watch him come home in his suit and leather shoes only to sink into his chair and demand dinner. I couldn't help but wonder what he could possibly be doing that caused him to stumble in the door and clutch his head every night. But when I did muff up the courage to ask him, he'd scoff and tell me it wasn't a lady's place to know.

"Business," he'd say, pointing his fork at me, "is a man's job. Always has been, always will be."

"Nah-uh. I can be a businessman if I want to, Dad," I fired back, sitting up on my knees to reach his height at the dinner table. As I stretched to meet him eye-to-eye, I could see the rage building in his eyes. He didn't like to be contradicted, especially by his daughter.

"Sweetie, no. Don't talk back. Be grateful that your father makes a good living for us," my mother jumped in, trying to cool the atmosphere as the vein in my father's neck began popping out. As I sat back in my chair, I picked my fork back up to pick at my potatoes.

"I'm not talking back. I'm just saying I could do it," I mumbled.

"No more discussion," he said, firmly.

My eyebrows furled as we sat in silence around the table. Suddenly, he slammed down his silverware, stood up quickly and exited the room. I heard him sink angrily into his favorite arm chair, striking a match as he did so. The grey smoke of his favorite cigar wafted into the room as my nose crinkled in response to the odor.

"May I be excused, Mom?" I questioned as politely as I could manage with gritted teeth. My lip quivered with frustration as I plastered a fake smile on my face.

"Go ahead, sweetie," my mom sighed, standing to clear the dishes.

I took a deep breath, regaining my composure before entering the family room. In the corner sat my father on his throne: feet up, chair reclined, cigar lit, and the newspaper unfolded in his hands. I didn't say anything as I calmly walked past him and picked up the paper from the night before. Opening the small drawer on the bookstand, I took out one prized, Cuban cigar and placed in my mouth. Somehow managing to balance the cigar in my teeth, I gathered the paper and loudly took a seat in the sofa right next to my father. I kicked off my slippers and put my feet up to rest on the ottoman as I unfolded the paper and turned to the section labeled "Business".

There we sat, in dead silence. I was awaiting an outburst, or even a smack with the paper, but I turned to meet the eyes of my father simply staring at me. He looked, up and down, at my small frame sitting proudly with the paper and a smoke. I saw him reach to take his cigar out to speak, but his hand stopped halfway up. Instead, he simply fluffed his paper and turned to continue reading. A smile hatched on my face as I saw him retreat. I had won.

It wasn't long before our newspaper readings became a routine, though he still gave me a grimace and look of disapproval from time to time. After each nightly reading of the business section, I grew envious of the people I read about. They were more than people, they were idols. I knew I would one day be so important that people would read about *me* in their nightly papers.

Over the years, I tried countless get-rich-quick schemes, all of which I thought were my big break. Gold jewelry, stocks, and bonds had slipped through my fingertips at the last second. Every rule of business I had learned from the paper, I had followed. Yet, it was these *things*, material things I had been blessed with for my whole life, that had failed me. My mind couldn't help but remember the countless times my mother would excuse my father's attitude as soon as he bought her a new dress. When I refuted his sexist claims, he'd tell me to be grateful for all the things he provided for me, gesturing at the crystalled clocks, embroidered curtains, and china plates that surrounded us.

I shook my head and sunk into the couch once more, settling into the same dent I had made from nights of endless reading. Reaching back to turn on the dim light, I grabbed another newspaper and propped it open. The front page revealed nothing new - the stock market, Wall Street, and the same tired headlines ran across the page. My exhausted eyes skimmed the words as I flipped carelessly, but my eye stopped suddenly upon a word I had never seen before: speakeasy. Squinting, I hunched over to make sense of the grainy picture. At what looked to be a bar, men sat with glasses full of alcohol. The man behind the bar held a stack of cash in his palm, which he was eagerly shoving into an open register.

I sat back as I felt the pieces slowly falling into place in my racing mind. Eagerly, I pulled on my slippers and ran to catch the elevator just outside my apartment.

"Floor three, please," I asked the bellman, a hint of urgency in my voice. The journey down from the twenty-third floor to the third was excruciatingly long. When I heard the buzzing of the elevator as it finally approached the familiar floor, I barely waited for the doors to open before I pushed myself through. Right across the hall stood Apt. Number 14. On the wooden door, I gave four quick knocks before Jack opened the door with an irritated look. His face was half shaven, his shirt half-unbuttoned, and the socks on his feet were ridden with holes. Instantly, he snapped to attention as he tried to button his tattered shirt. A greasy hand reached to comb through his messy hair as he stood up straight. His mouth opened to ask me why I was on his doorstep in my pajamas, but I stopped him before he could comment.

"You wanna make a lot of money?" I said, leaning against the door frame and faking a cool expression.

Though he put on an irritated face, I could see a spark of curiosity in his eyes as I flashed him the headline of the paper. Upon reading it, he rolled his eyes as he went back to slouching and biting his nails.

"Jack, come on," I whined.

"Kathryn, how many times are you gonna have one of these bright ideas and try to drag me into it? You and your opportunities are gonna get you in a lot of trouble," he said, shaking his head at the paper.

"But Jack, I have a good feeling about this one," I said.

"You always have a good feeling, Kat," he responded.

"You haven't even read the article," I said, pushing it into his face.

Rolling his eyes, he took the paper from my hands and sank into his stained chair. He skimmed the paper as his mouth twisted into a distressed squiggle.

As I waited for him to finish the article, I looked around his once tidy apartment. I saw dirty dishes piled in his rusting sink, curtains hanging off half broken rods, and a layer of cigarette butts gracing the wooden floor. Empty whiskey and gin bottles lined the counter from months prior. Small scraps of paper covered in his messy scrawl were strewn around the room. Noticing he was now deep in the article, I bent over quietly to pick up one of the many wads. On it was scribbled countless numbers and calculations. Looking closer, I could decipher the few dollar signs on the page and a single world: savings. A furiously written zero was etched under the arithmetic.

Glancing back to him, sunken defeatedly into the sofa, I could see the same face of the poor boy who would come over to play every afternoon. The thrill I felt when I heard the quick four raps on my apartment door that let me know he was there. The hours that we spent lost in our own imaginations, creating the lives we were always dreaming of. For me, it was the business I longed to build. But for him, it was a life of wealth. It was the silver watches and expensive suits that my father wore every day but never thought twice about. I could see the jealousy on his face every time he stepped through our door.

As we played one day, I remembered seeing a patchy hole in the knee of his pants.

"What's that?" I said, pointing and laughing. He looked down, hesitantly, as he noticed the rip himself.

"It's nothin', Kat. Leave it alone," he said, pushing my hand away.

"Why dontcha just get new ones?" I questioned, poking my fingers through the fabric again.

"Leave it alone!" he cried, now slapping away my hand. As I looked closer at his face, I could see a small silver tear running down his cheek. I had never seen a boy cry before. His bottom lip trembled as he reached up to wipe at his eyes.

"I'm sorry," I mumbled, clasping my hands in my lap and looking down. He sat, still hunched over, saying nothing. "I'll fix it, I promise,"

I said, now pleading for him to give me any response; but, he remained silent.

Abruptly, I stood and ran to my father's room. Behind the opened closet door hung a row of freshly pressed suits, fitted with gold buttons and a silk pocket square. On my tiptoes, I reached to pull a suit off of one of the hangers above before rushing back into the family room.

"Here," I said, tossing the suit on his lap. He looked up, an expression of confusion on his face. Looking back down at the jacket, his hands traced the buttons, taking in every small detail etched on their surfaces. "Just try it," I urged, gesturing for him to stand up.

As he pulled on the navy pants over his ripped corduroys, his familiar smile began growing again. I held open the jacket as he slipped into it, his small arms not even reaching halfway down the length of the sleeves. "Now look," I smiled, pulling him into the view of the mirror in the corner of the room. The pant legs dragged on the ground as he trudged to take a look at himself.

Instantly, he adjusted his posture and smoothed the shoulder pads as he posed. He let out a small chuckle as he continued to look at himself proudly.

"Thanks, Kat," he said, still keeping his eyes glued to the mirror.

"You can keep it," I said, beaming. "My father won't notice one out of his million suits is missing," I reasoned.

"No, I can't," he frowned, turning back to look at me for the first time since he had put on the suit.

"Yes you can," I nodded. "Please?" I smiled sweetly. His once serious expression grew into a full-fledged grin as he reached out to embrace me.

"Thanks, Kat," he cried, gripping me tight in a hug. My heart flip-flopped as I felt his arms around me. Suddenly, his face dipped down as he left a small kiss on my cheek, leaving my own face flushed red.

As I looked back to him now, still sitting in his broken chair, I longed to make his face light up just as it did on that day. Quietly, I walked over to stand behind him.

"Just think Jack," I continued, wrapping my arms around his broad shoulders.

"You and me. We go fifty-fifty -" I persisted.

"Alright, alright, Kat. You got it. But this is the last one. I'm not falling for your sweet talking, or those big eyes, or -" I cut him off with a quick kiss.

"You're the best, love!" I called over my shoulder as I ran towards the creaking elevator once more.

In six short months, we managed to build up one of Manhattan's biggest speakeasies in the music district. Jack's friend had rented us a room for real cheap in the basement of a now vacant apartment building. Amidst the cobwebs and rats' nests, we fashioned a wooden bar, complete with makeshift barstools. On the far side, Jack constructed a slanted but usable stage for our nightly entertainment. In massive metal buckets opposite the stage, he and his buddies, soon to be our bartenders, would mix huge batches of murky malt liquors and grainy beers to be sold. Though Jack and his friends made the alcohol, none of it was sold before passing my inspection. Every night, they lined up neatly behind their barrels as they waited eagerly for my approval. As I walked down the line, I dipped my small glass into each bucket and took a sip of every pungent mix.

Though I was usually satisfied with their products, I couldn't help but lose my temper from time to time. Sometimes, the beer was too grainy. Other times, the liquor was so strong that it was undrinkable; but ever since one bartender had made the mistake of spilling an entire bucket of alcohol, they were careful not to let me down again.

As I saw and smelt the liquid running across the room that day, my face grew flushed with rage. I could practically see the profit we could have made laying on the floor.

"Who did this?" I yelled, my fists clenching in anger. The only response I received was their bodies frozen in place and their faces in shock from my raised voice. "Now! I want to know who spilt this entire bucket!" I screeched, slamming my fist on the countertop. Still, they were silent.

"Jack?" I called, trying to keep my voice calm.

"Yes, Kat," he said, keeping his head down.

"You tell me right now who did this," I breathed, tapping my foot impatiently. He paused as he looked around nervously at his buddies. "I'm waiting," I said, an edge in my voice.

He sighed as he finally gave in. "He did," he mumbled, pointing across the bar at one of his old high school friends.

"Okay. You can go now," I said to the culprit.

"I can go?" he scoffed. "I spilt one bucket, Kat. Gimme a break," he whined, picking up a full glass and taking a sip nonchalantly.

Slowly, I stepped towards him as he took another drink. As he tipped back the cup to get the last drop, I grabbed the glass from his hands and threw it to the ground. The glass shattered on the already splintering floor.

"I said you can go now," I repeated, staring coldly at him. Suddenly, his brow furled in realization. Quietly but hurriedly, he shuffled to the other side of the room and grabbed his coat, pulling it over his shoulders. Though he gave a defiant *hmph* as he exited, I could see the defeated look on his face. As I looked back at the other boys, they stood up straighter when my head faced their direction.

"The rest of you are fine. Get ready for a busy rush hour tonight," I said, turning again. From that night on, no drop of alcohol had ever been spilt again.

Despite my optimistic demeanor and booming business, there was change creeping through the streets of Manhattan lately. The tension that spread like flames throughout the city had been extinguished as speakeasies were shut down daily. I began to worry each time the newspaper headline read *New Speakeasy Busted in Downtown Manhattan*. Even the powerful businessmen I had once looked upon admiringly as a child were shown behind bars, their businesses stamped out like old cigarette butts. I ran my hands over the wrinkled page, licking my fingertip to turn each one. On the backside was another picture from the latest Wall Street corruption scandal. Even in the mug shot, he was still dressed like every other rich businessman in the city. A deep suit, shining buttons, and a striped pocket square was tucked neatly into the pocket; his face was clearly distraught, judging from the deep, sunken eyes that rested below his deep frown lines. His mouth bore no smile, but rather a grimace and look of irritation. Looking closer at the picture, the grimace on the man's face looked too familiar. The protruding neck vein and furled brow were a dead giveaway.

Somewhat in shock, I sat back in my chair to make sense of what lay in front of me. I had never seen my father look as defeated as he did right now.

"Kat, you okay?" I heard a sloppy voice behind me ask. Jack spun me around and placed a cigarette in my teeth.

"Yeah, yeah. I'm fine, love," I said, faking enthusiasm. With shaking hands, he passed me another drink. One hand held mine while his other clung to his whiskey. As we swayed to the music, I struck a match and lit the end. As we danced, Jack mumbled along made up words to the song blasting from the band.

I was startled, however, by a strange knock on the door. The music came to a halt as the conversation fizzled out. The image of my father with his glare of disappointment still stung in my mind as I grew paranoid with remembrance of the headlines I had read earlier.

With the lightest drunken steps he could manage, Jack stepped to the door, careful not to reveal his face through the small window. I could hear the trembling breaths of every person in the room. The thick tension was stagnant in the air. I knew that each pair of eyes could see the ominous shadow of the figure outside, projected onto the wall Jack was leaning against. Holding my breath, I shuddered as I heard the doorknob rattling. Two squinting eyes peeked through the door's peephole as Jack slid down, hoping to be out of sight. His rubber soles let out a small squeak as he sunk to the cement floor. My eyes shut, and my head bowed. My shaking hands clutched each other in an attempt to keep them from fluttering.

It wasn't until the figure backed away, timidly, that I could breathe a sigh of relief. It was cut short, however, by the sound of shattering glass. Looking back, I saw the face of our bartender as he realized the consequences of his mistake. On the ground laid a puddle of amber liquid amidst shards of crystal.

With one thunderous crack, the lock on our door fell to the floor, defeated. The one unknown figure multiplied into an army of men with guns drawn.

"Who runs this?" the officer yelled.

Not a word was said as we froze in our places. The officer raised his gun higher and his voice louder as he grew irritated.

"*Now,*" he said sternly, his glare bearing no sense of mercy.

I looked up to lock eyes with the sneering barrel of the pistol aimed in my direction. I had become just like my father, alright. I would be seeing him too soon if I didn't come up with a plan fast.

Come on, Kat. I racked my brain for any scheme I had learned from my nights of reading, but my mind was blank. I gulped as I prepared to step forward, but I felt the familiar strength of a hand pushing me back.

"Me!" he cried. "Please don't shoot. Please! Here," I heard Jack's still drunk voice echoing from behind me as he wobbled out to meet the officer.

As he surrendered his wrists in front of him, two sturdy cuffs closed around them. I watched in disbelief as my Jack was tied up and led away. The other officers scattered about the room, pushing through the crowd while digging through our elaborate setup. The unmistakable odor of alcohol reeked from the corner of the room as it spilled out of its barrels. Customers I once saw as my most loyal fans left me stranded as they bolted out the door. Why were they leaving without worrying about me? Had they forgotten about me?

Trying to pull myself back to reality, I pushed my hands through my greasy bob. My forehead was coated in a cold sweat. I blinked rapidly as if I just needed to clear away a film from my eyes and it would only be a bad dream I was experiencing.

But Jack? Where was he now? My dilated eyes caught only a glimpse of him struggling against the grip of the burly police officer as they lead him out of the room. As I collapsed back into the wooden chair, I watched as just another one of my opportunities slipped through my fingertips at the last second. And this time, it took Jack with it.

The trek on the pitch black streets had become so routine that it was almost comfortable tonight. The small window of time I had meant I had to hurry: only an hour to visit was usually permitted on Fridays. As I passed 45th Street and saw the too familiar wrought iron gate, I shuffled along with even more haste. Shaking my head, I swore I could still hear the echo of jazz music. I reached the somber gate in record time, gracing the four marble steps to the entrance in my heels with ease. Swinging open the stone door, I was greeted by the oddly cheery face of the receptionist.

"Back again, dear?" she said, smiling.

I didn't have to say anything for her to know who I was here for. I simply nodded and forced a half smile before the buzzer rang and another cold door popped open. My hands clenched into a polite fold and rested on my freshly ironed skirt. My eyes stared down at my broken wristwatch to watch the seconds hiccupping by as I adjusted my position in the rigid metal chair. From my bag, I pulled out last night's newspaper, turning to the business section as always. I kept my eyes on the paper to distract myself from the dark bags that collected under his eyes and his tall frame swallowed by the orange suit. Today, though, the headline of *Another Speakeasy Busted in Tin Pan Alley* made me shut it instantly. My head snapped up as I heard the clink from behind the glass in front of me.

"Hey, doll."

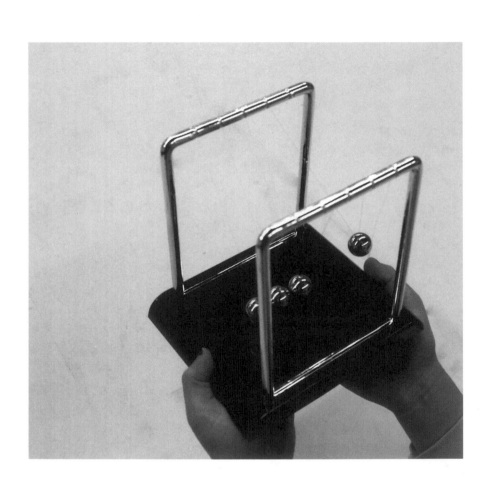

The Significance of Time

The high-pitched shriek of bagpipes filled the air and bounced from building to building. A drumroll followed, and the loud cracking seemed to silence the friends and family of one of New York's bravest. The casket was blanketed with an American flag. The red stripes showed Crimson red blood from all who ran in when everyone else was running out. The field of blue was as crisp now as the September morning that made history and made the world stop turning for those five hours. The crying and sobbing seemed endless- like a waterfall that was constantly flowing. Wives who expected their husbands home for dinner that night, children who would have to grow up without their fathers and never play catch in the front yard, brothers who were like best friends- all gone in what seemed to be just the blink of an eye. Church bells echoed through the city and hundreds of uniformed men lined the streets.

Johnny rolled out of bed and rubbed the sleep out of his eyes; a decent night's sleep was rare while working the graveyard shift. The smell of greasy, crisp bacon filled the halls of the fire house as Johnny made his way down the hall.

"Morning Chief, how's the back today, got a good night sleep for once, huh?" Sal greeted. "I'm getting too old for this, Sally boy, when I wake up in the morning everything hurts!" he replied. Laughter filled the kitchen as Johnny entered.

"Morning Chief", the crew exclaimed as they set the table for breakfast, as one of the guys continued his banter.

The kitchen was always a place where our family gathered. Not the family back at home, but the family of guys that made up Rescue Company 1. No matter what kind of shit was thrown at us each day, we could always count on some good food, laughs, and help from the brothers back in the kitchen. Johnny gathered the guys around the table for breakfast and started going over their day's assignments. Johnny threw his newspaper down on the table that read September 11th 2001 in bold black letters and made his way to the coffee machine for his morning cup.

Liam entered the kitchen wearing a sleek, custom suit carrying the day's edition of the New York Times. His beautiful wife and son were eating breakfast. The bright September sun painted the hardwood floors of their penthouse dwelling as it rose over the river and the hundreds of other buildings that dotted the city skyline.

"I made Michael chocolate pancakes darling, would you like some? They're your favorite," Callie asked.

"No thanks," Liam said as he exited the room, his face buried in his phone. Callie shrugged her shoulders and shook her head.

"I guess that means there are more for us!"

Michael smiled as Liam's cell phone began to vibrate the counter- a daily occurrence, the annoying buzzing seemed to be a daily routine throughout breakfast.

"Honey, have you seen my watch?" Liam yelled from up the stairs.

"On the dresser," Callie replied.

The click, clack of his leather dress shoes filled the foyer; Liam darted into the kitchen and kissed Michael and Callie goodbye. Liam gazed into Callie's ocean blue eyes, she leaned over and kissed her husband goodbye and hesitated to make conversation before she was interrupted by that constant ringing.

"Go, have a great day, love you," she said with a sad tone as she watched her husband leave for work.

Liam first met Callie their first year of college. He was a finance major and she was studying international business. She thought he was very sweet and he would always go out of his way to make her feel special. He would buy her flowers and they would go on dates often. The couple loved to go on road trips and travel any opportunity they had.. Upon graduation Liam got a job with the New York Stock exchange. He worked very hard and spent many evenings staring at his computer screen. He would work very hard but the couple had a beautiful wedding and bought a luxurious house which started their life together.

The job certainly changed him; he wasn't the same Liam she met years ago.

"Michael, go get dressed and get ready for school," Liam grabbed the warm bagel that his wife left for him and he slammed the door shut. He made his way down the cobblestone driveway where a jet black Escalade was waiting for him. He opened the door and was greeted by his driver. "Good morning, Mr.O'Ryan," looking into the rear view mirror. Liam continued to prepare for his work day without any acknowledgement.

Johnny was sitting in his office that overlooked the truck floor. He saw the guys laughing as they dumped the water bucket on one of the new guys who happened to be cleaning the rigs. Johnny reached over and banged on the glass window. All three of the guys looked up and stopped their antics trying to hold back their smirking faces and laughs as they got back to cleaning the rigs. Johnny smiled; he could remember his first year on the job. The older guys would play pranks and harass him about everything, but it was all part of the job and the tradition. Anyone who has worked in the fire service, could tell you that the guys are just a bunch of big kids who haven't fully grown up. At that moment, Johnny was snapped into reality. A bright yellow banner flashed over the television stating breaking news. A live image depicted one of the World Trade Towers bellowing thick black smoke which rolled over the New York skyline. Someone captured a video of a plane crashing into the building from the streets and the news reports flooded in. The radio came to life as emergency personnel responded to the disaster. Full box alarms were issued as trucks, engines, and S.O.C companies were all requested to respond. The piercing alarm burst through loudspeakers. The voice from dispatch crackled over the alarm system.

"All FDNY units report to the North Tower off of West Street, reported plane crash smoke and visible flames on the 93rd floor!"

Doors flung open and the crew piled into the garage.

"We got a big job today fellas, time to put on the big boy pants!"

Black turnout pants sprung to life as the guys jumped into them, pulling the bright colored elastic suspenders over their shoulders, saddling up for what would prove to be a very trying day. Coats were haphazardly thrown into the rigs as doors began slamming shut, with the men inside the trucks ready to head to the scene. As the hum of the rig met the ears of the men inside, the roar of the engine shook the concrete floor of the garage as the large door came to life, flying up, illuminating the street that the trucks began to pull out onto.

Johnny ran out to the truck floor jumping into the fly car. He pulled out into the hustle and bustle and flicked on the lights and sirens, which echoed from building to building. Johnny felt a gut wrenching knot in his stomach, as a bead of sweat trickled down his forehead. He had felt this feeling many times before but it was the part of his love for the job. Immediately he began trying to prepare for the job that lie ahead. *Were there people trapped? Has a engine accessed the fire do we have water?* Johnny kept running through these thoughts in his mind until the radio crackled.

"Traffic is bad Chief, our ETA is 15 minutes!"

Johnny laid on the horn and cars slowly crept to the right.

"10-4, following a block behind, see you in 15," replied Johnny. Evacuate, Extinguish, Exit, these same three thoughts ran through his mind as he forced his way down the crowded streets of lower Manhattan.

👁 👁

"I told you three freakin' times that you needed to get those papers signed. I don't care what you have to do- they will be on my desk by this afternoon or I will leave the discharge paperwork on yours…. I don't need another excuse. Do your job, it's that simple or I can get any bum on the New York City streets to do it," Liam hung up the phone and looked down at his watch furious.

The Escalade was stopped at a red light as a crowd of people crossed the street in front of them. The light turned green and the great wave of people kept crossing. Looking down at his Submariner Rolex, it sparkled with the same shine that it had the day he received it from his parents.

A sea of black covered the courtyard where the students were all sitting as they were anxiously awaiting their names to be called, myself included. The Valedictorian of our class finished his speech and proclaimed his well wishes. One of my professors stepped up to the podium and began announcing names. His maroon robe and funny hat showed true to the colors of Fordham University. Greg Olsen.... John O'Rourke.... Liam O'Ryan." As they called my name, screams and clapping filled the air. The warm spring breeze touched my face as I made my way to collect my diploma. I don't think there was a happier day in my life. I was going to miss this place, some of the best years of my life were spent partying and going to school here. The sun was so bright and the feelings of hope and success filled the crowd of students. The professor reached out to shake my hand. "Well done son!" I smiled, shook my head and left the stage looking out over hundreds of people hoping to see my parents. I'm sure they were just as happy as I was. "Congratulations Fordham Class of 1997!" I took off my cap and threw it into the sky and the crowd of students started cheering. I walked up the hill to the oak tree where my parents were. They greeted me with large smiles, and my mom reached out for a big hug. Your father and I are so proud of you, Liam. Dad shook my hand, "good work kid." My mom went into her purse and pulled out a jewelry box. "We got you something for all your hard work," she exclaimed. I opened the box and my jaw almost dropped. "A Rolex... WOW thank you guys so much, I love you!" It sparkled in the sun, the navy blue rim showed intricate detail, and there were gold pieces that told time. Right now, it was time to spend with family and make my parents proud. I couldn't thank them enough. "Every business man needs a watch," said dad! CLICK, flash, a photographer had snapped a picture.

The time read 8:15 and they were still stuck at the traffic light waiting for all the people to cross. The light turned red again and Liam flipped. "Can anyone ever do their job," he screamed. Liam grabbed his leather briefcase and threw his papers inside out of frustration.

"So sorry, Mr. O'Ryan."

"No, you will be sorry when I call your boss," he retorted.

Liam got out of the vehicle and slammed the door shut. The warm autumn breeze bit his freshly shaven face and he decided to start walking. The buildings towered above the busy streets touching the sun that was like a blanket covering the city. Liam continued to walk for about a block and decided to hail a cab. Throwing his arm in the air, a cab pulled over as he opened the door.

"11 Wall Street and maybe the nearest CVS so you can get some deodorant," Liam ordered, scrunching his nose at the car's smell.

Liam looked outside at all the people who seemed to be of panic and thought about his wife and son. Amidst his thoughts and chaos his phone began to buzz. For the rest of the ride, Liam was on the phone with one of his clients from Long Island.

"Here is your stop, sir," the driver said with a thick accent.

Liam took out a $50 dollar bill and threw it at the cab driver. "Use the money to take a shower. You reek of BO!"

The driver was yelling something as he exited the car to the New York Stock Exchange with an American flag in the front of the building swaying in the breeze. In the distance, sirens began to fill the air, growing louder by the second. Liam walked across the street where a large crowd was gathered outside. He crossed the street and headed to the front door, glancing at his which shimmered in the morning sun.

A plane flew overhead which seemed to scrape right above the buildings. The deafening sound of the engine drowned out the commotion from the large crowd. People began pushing through the crowd and NYPD officers tried to control the stampede.

"What the hell is going on?" Liam asked a bystander.

"I heard a plane crashed into one of the towers at the World Trade Center," the man replied.

Five police officers opened the door and screams rang out from the crowd as a huge boom shocked the city.

"The Stock Exchange is closed today, everybody must leave this area until further notice!"

The six officers started barricading the exchange. People tried to push past, but were only stopped. Buzzing and ringtones filled the air and the crowd broke into chaos.

"Good morning this is your principal, Mr. Johnson. New York City today we will be having an early dismissal a large accident has occurred downtown and the city has requested that there be an early dismissal. Follow the instructions of your teachers and enjoy the rest of your day," Mr. Johnson said with a shaky hesitant voice

The loudspeaker went quiet. Mrs. Moran went over to her computer, her face showed a horrific expression as she gathered herself together. One of the teachers from across the hall popped her head in the room. The class continued with their morning workshop. Some were learning how to add and subtract while other students were tracing their names in cursive.

"Okay class, let's pack up our bags for dismissal and you guys can talk quietly."

The teacher walked the class down the hallway to the exit where nervous parents were already waiting. Many of their faces stricken with fear as they chattered away on their flip phones and messaging devices. Michael spotted his father ran towards him. He

"Hi Mrs. Moran, I'm here to pick up Michael!"

"Yes, thank you, have a good day get home safely," she said as they headed toward the car where their driver was waiting in the black Escalade.

"How was school kiddo?" Liam asked as he turned to his son.

"Why are we getting out so early?" Michael asked.

At that moment fire truck came hauling down the street flashing its lights and sirens.

Johnny pulled the SUV behind one of the rigs next to the North tower, and struggled to put his turnout jacket and helmet in the front

seat of the truck. Looking outside the truck, he saw the debris falling from the sky. Sal's voice came over the radio.

"Chief, we're inside the lobby near the Charlie side stairwell."

Johnny got out of the vehicle and walked towards the entrance to the North Tower.

"10-4, I'll meet you in two, " the chief replied.

He looked up, and saw black smoke and fire pouring of the gaping hole that the plane left. People seemed to be scrambling in and out of the building as the police attempted to stabilize and evacuate the area. Sal entered the tower and the flood of people filled the main hall. There were EMTs and Medics attending to the wounded, firefighters bringing down people in wheel chairs only to return back to the stairwell to make the climb. Hundreds of radios crackled with a sound of urgency and panic behind them. The morning sun poured in the famous arch windows and the world seemed to move in slow motion. Sal motioned for the crew to form around the Chief.

"I want two groups of four, our goal is to evacuate the entire building starting from the top, we all know there are people up there, let's get them out. Evacuation is our first priority, lookout for your brothers and stay safe. Group one, take the south side stairwell, group two, take the north side stairwell. Stay in contact with me at all times, we do this thing as a team."

Both teams headed toward the stairs as people covered in debris came rushing out. That gut wrenching knot in his stomach seemed to fade as he began leading his team. Johnny. The ground started to shake a Johnny lost his balance and fell to his knees as people around him started to scream. A thunderous rumble, the likeness of one thousand freight trains, shook the building. The sky outside turned black. Some glass windows broke and large pieces of metal peppered the ground. Johnny grabbed the radio and called to his men.

"The South Tower just collapsed! Be very careful and get your asses back down here as soon as possible!" No response was heard and the lobby was frantic.

Johnny started helping people in this location. Those who were in critical condition were cared for first. Johnny stabilized the lobby in the matter of minutes. He called support from his teams and waited for a response, but nothing came through. In the middle of instructing some medics from a company up town, one of the new guys, Jerry from group A, came over to him.

"Have you guys heard my messages over the radio?" Johnny asked in a pissed off tone.

"No sir, our guys are up top fighting through the smoke and flames to get to some trapped victims, we missed the message," said Jerry.

"Jerry I want you to go back up and tell them to make their way back down evacuating each floor below 93, I will take the other staircase and meet group B."

Jerry left for the stairwell as Johnny headed off in the opposite direction. He opened the door and began to make the long climb. The floor beneath Johnny's feet began to vibrate and rumble.

"I can't get a hold of mom right now, the connection is not so great, I'm sure she is at home worried sick. We need to call grandma and grandpa when we get home," Liam told his son.

"Daddy why did we get out of school so early?" Michael asked.

The cars dotted the dotted the bridge like a thousand ants trying to cram into an anthill. Cars crammed and honked all fighting to get across the bridge as quickly as possible. Liam took a deep breath and looked into his son's curious eyes. He told his son years later about some very bad men in a faraway lands. These men didn't like the American people and had different beliefs. Michaels dad explained how they wanted to do bad things to good people, and crashing the planes into the buildings was their way of doing that.

"Michael," he said, " I love you very, very much and nothing bad will happen to you, those men who did this will pay for their actions," he stated in an angry tone.

The two looked out over the river and the we could see the smoke filling the sky. Two fire trucks passed us on the opposite side of the bridge. An American flag flying proudly behind them and the number 903 was listed on the back. Michael could tell that his father was scared and told him about his day at school and writers workshop and our summer story. Liam looked at Michael and smiled. During that time he did not glance at his phone one time. Liam looked out the window back at the city as they merged off the bridge. Only one tower was standing and a cloud of smoke blanketed the city the same way the sun had that morning. Liam looked down at his watch and noticed a large cracked streaked down the face of his face.

The sparkly watch stopped reading time at 9:03 am, dust and shards of glass were protruding. Liam was quiet for the rest of the ride home and Michael noticed a few tears rolling down his cheek that day. The two finally made it home where Cali was waiting on the front steps with Liam's mother, their faces showed sorrow and exhaustion. Liam spent a minute speaking to the driver and thanking him for the ride as Cali came over and squeezed Michael in a tight hug. The black Escalade pulled out of the driveway and Liam came over to us and gave us all a big hug.

"I love you!"

Michael woke up rubbing the sleep out of his eyes. "Michael, take a shower and get dressed, we need to leave in one hour honey!"

I got out of the shower and Calli was waiting with a nice shirt and some fancy black clothes like his father always wore to work. She helped him get dressed and ready. A big plate of chocolate chip pancakes was waiting for Michael downstairs which he devoured. "Liam, it's time to go, we'll meet you in the car," his mom called upstairs. The three of us waited outside, for a long time. "I'll go inside and get him Callie," Michael's grandmother stated. The two of them returned to the car and we headed off. The family crossed that same bridge they took everyday, but there was something missing. The car ride was silent. The four arrived at the church and pulled in behind a line of black cars like ours, uniformed men lined the streets. The warm September sun shined brightly and the clear blue sky stretched for miles. The high-pitched shriek of bagpipes filled the air and bounced from building to building. A drumroll followed, and the loud crack seemed to silence the crowd. A fire truck carrying some sort of large box covered with an American flag slowly crept toward the entrance to the church.

Tears trickled down the faces of Michael's parents and his grandmother started to weep. Liam helped the uniformed men carry the flag box off the fire truck and into the church as the crowd of people followed. Liam's jet black outline could be seen kneeling, his head buried in his arms at the front of the church. Liam slammed the watch down on the coffin, it was sparkling with the same shine it had many years ago. Callie left her seat to retrieve Liam from the altar.

On Michaels 18th birthday he found a jewelry box sitting next to a manila envelope. He opened the envelope to find a card addressed to him by his father. Inside the envelope was a picture of Michael, his dad, and his grandfather. The card was inscribed with a message from his father.

Happy 18th Birthday Michael.

The most priceless thing in this world is time and time is something we can not seem to ever have enough of. Make the most of the time you have and continue to make us proud. Every man needs his watch!
Love, Dad

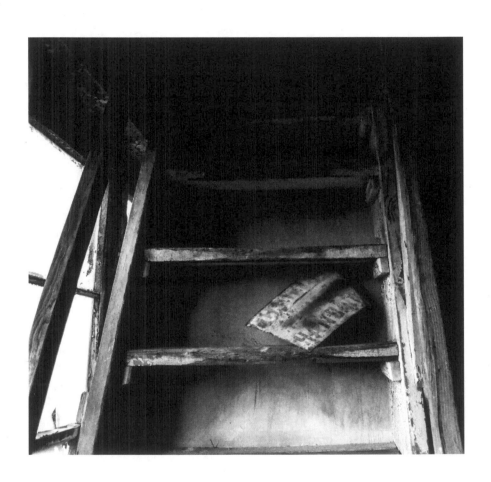

A Cure for Hope

The harsh cracking of glass beneath heavy boots echoed throughout the tavern. It was an average street corner bar, the kind that could be found every few blocks in urban areas, however this particular bar was in shambles. Old tables stretched across the floor, flat screen TVs that once mounted the walls now laid strewn on the ground, and a thin layer of broken glass coated the floor and counters. I pushed two fallen barstools from my path and vaulted over the counter. My expectations were low, but not nearly low enough to keep me from trying. Scouring up and down the wall, my eyes wandered, like a patient hunter searching for a potential kill. After a brief moment, my eyebrows faintly rose up, and I reached to grab the amber-colored bottle; Jack Daniels, untouched, hidden behind a plank of wood once fitted to the ceiling. A grin stretched across my face for the first time in a long while as I muttered "Bingo," beneath my breath and snatched the bottle. A sheet of dust glazed its exterior, and as I brushed it off, I could feel the smooth, brisk glass underneath. I made my way out of the tavern, slowly losing my grin and the faint happiness I had felt just moments ago with the city back in my sight once again. Birds could be heard chirping from outside, joined by a slight breeze to make up the only eternal noise that could be heard. *Back to the real world*, I thought, crunching glass beneath my feet and the shimmering reflection of the setting sun emanating off the remaining windows.

❧ ❧

It had been over five years since I'd seen a real face other than mine. If it weren't for the plethora of countenances plastered all over New York on billboards and magazines, I would have probably forgotten that people once existed all together. Yet the various faces of celebrities, models, and political figures remained a constant reminder of the past- back when people were still around. And despite this, all these reminders did nothing to help me remember what was important: the faces of my family.

I used to wonder why my coworkers always carried around pictures of their kids or significant others in their wallets. In a way, it felt like overkill. I was a firm believer that there was no point in keeping pictures if you came home to see them everyday. I would always catch a glimpse of my co-workers' kids every time they pulled out their wallets, whether it be at happy hour or when I was sent with them to get lunch for everybody back at the building. Were they trying to brag? 'Hey, look at my kids, look how amazing they are, I created them.' Or something to that effect. I just found it to be pretentious. Nevertheless, that luxury was now gone, and there hadn't been a single waking moment I haven't regretted not doing this one simple task. It could've been so easy. The kids always got a ton of wallet sized pictures when we ordered photos from the school. Yet, for some odd reason, I felt as if having their pictures in my wallet meant that I wouldn't come home to see them, that I'd go for a lengthy period of time without them. Kind of ironic when you think about it. Regretting not doing the one thing that I subconsciously thought would lead to my current situation. Well, joke's on me, because I can't remember my own damn kids' faces. What I wouldn't give to see them again. Hear them again. Anything.

If doctors were still around, I would most definitely have been classified as clinically insane. Even with my very apparent minimal amount of background information in psychology, I was fairly certain my self-diagnosis was at least semi-accurate. Hallucinations, delusions, and sudden losses of memory were all daily occurrences. My morning routine usually consisted of waking with a sudden jolt, shortly forgetting where I was, promptly followed by a few minutes of prolonged vomiting. I would then check the ham radio sitting a few feet from my mattress, situated on a small table alongside my handgun. I didn't even know why I still use the old thing. It had been over four years since I had found the bulky radio, and in all those years I had never been able to make contact with anybody or receive a signal back. Yet every day, I found myself spending hours sitting on the roof of the same skyscraper with the thing hooked up to an antenna just listening to static. I would broadcast my name and location a few times every hour in hopes that somebody may hear it and either contact me back or show up here, but nobody ever did. Just static. *Always* just static.

Before my unfortunate isolation, back when everything was normal, I lived in Long Island with my wife, Jessica, and two children, Noah and Madison. We lived a quiet and normal suburban life, the kind seen in movies and things alike. I worked as a pipeline engineer and took the train to Grand Central every weekday morning. It was a simple life, and even though my job kept me from being home often, I tried my hardest to make the best of it when I was, but sometimes your hardest isn't enough. Working weekends and staying late was frequently becoming more normal. In an attempt to make up for the lack of time with my kids, I attempted to bring them gifts whenever I could- take them to the movies or treat them with trips to the local amusement park from time to time. Madison and Noah's favorite 'dad activity' was going out for ice cream, and I would oblige a bit more often than I should, despite my wife persisting that I was influencing them to live an unhealthy lifestyle, which would lead to confrontations in the grocery store, albeit lighthearted confrontations.

"Beat you again," I'd say with a smirk across my face.

"Yeah, yeah, yeah, whatever. I like to take my time, find deals and stuff. You just want to get in and get out." I would lift Madison from the cart onto the floor so she could give Mommy a hug.

"Who wants to be stuck in this place for longer than they need to?" Jessica walked over to the cart, kissed Noah on the forehead while ruffling Madison's already messy hair, and picked up a box of yogurts.

"This is the kinda thing I'm talking about. You know how much sugar is in just one of these?" she asked. "The kids like 'em." I shrugged.

"The kids also like you too, doesn't mean you're good for them," she joked, a smile widening across her face. She threw the box back to me and told Madison and Noah this was just special treat.

It was the little things that made me fall for her more and more everyday.

147

She used to go to the gym religiously before the kids, but had to give it up for the sake of Madison and Noah since I was usually at work and the kids hated the child care center the gym provided. They much preferred to stay home and play with the neighborhood kids or use the video game system we had bought them for Christmas. Noah usually hogged it, always claiming that video games were for boys. Then they would get into a fight that I'd have to break up because Jessica typically ignored them. She seemed awfully tired for being a stay-at-home mom, but the more I thought about it, the more I realized how much of a handful those two were- in a good way, though- she was a good mom.

My mind snapped back from my daydream. I found myself looking over the horizon at the sunset. Buildings stretched up to the clouds surrounded by a green sea of vegetation. With a lack of people inhabiting the city, animals began to repopulate the streets. Plants and grass had become overgrown and the blocks were filled with roaming herds of curious deer. It was strange, but it felt almost normal now. After gathering myself, I made my way back to the setup and laid back in the chair, sipping an amber liquid from the dusty bottle. I coughed, wiped my lips, and took another sip. It had been ages since my last drink. The constant humming of white noise was a painful reminder of my isolation. It meant that nobody was listening, or that somebody was and just wasn't responding. Why I subjected myself to this torture, I didn't know. And yet, I found myself up there everyday, waiting. All I knew was that I had to keep going.

There was something calming about the silent city's skyline if I tuned out the static. It was a phenomenon I thought I'd never see: the city that never sleeps taking a long deserved rest.

The building was located only a few blocks away from my company's HQ building, or rather, what used to be the HQ building. I had passed it everyday on my way to work, never imagining that I'd spend so much time there in the future. It was a large studio that broadcasted a couple of stations to the tri-state area using the towering antenna situated on the roof.

My thoughts remained stagnant, hoping a bit of alcohol could possibly jog my memory of a few goods times with friends or family. Over the years, my mind eroded into a blank, unmoving consciousness. The days were always the same: loot, wait, sleep- every single day.

Looting was important and was the reason why I survived for so long. It's how I managed to find food and basic necessities, along with the radio, generator, and the gun. Even though most grocery stores were in shambles, five years of looting for one man barely dents a city's resources.

The sun was sinking over the horizon. I took another drink. It was the same sunset I viewed every evening. On the same rooftop I sat on every day. Listening to the same static. Sitting in the same chair. And through it all, I was still alone.

My thoughts trailed back to the day it happened. Taking work off that day would've been great. The kids had the day off from school and I had woken up with a slight headache. I told a half-awake Jessica this, and she lazily rolled over, flopped her arm on me, and buried her face into my side.

"Just don't go in, we can lie around all day and do nothing."

I chuckled as I picked up her arm from my chest and leaned up.

"I wish. They got some pipe in the lower east side that needs to be checked out, some old water line like six hundred feet down."

She made a pouty face as I strolled toward the bathroom.

"Besides, we wouldn't be able to lie around all day. Madison's got that haircut at two and your parents wanted to stop by later to give Noah his present," I said as she let out a loud sigh and rolled onto her back.

The elevator ride took a lot longer than I thought. 600 feet feels a lot deeper when it's descending at the pace of a drunken snail. The air gradually felt more moist the further we went down, as if we were in some cave under a waterfall. I was part of a team of five people, including myself. One of the guys, Gary, was claustrophobic, but kept it to himself for the most part. I could tell since he stayed in the middle of the elevator, unmoving with the exception of slight shaking. Looking around, I could tell the others noticed it too. A good friend of mine, Sarah, went up to him and put her hand on his shoulder. He flinched, almost like he snapped out of a trance he put himself into as a distraction from our descent. "You're fine Gary, relax." He turned to her, then to the rest of us, and sighed.

"How old is this goddamn elevator? Why are they still using these old pipes? I don't know why they need me down here, I work in the office." She shrugged. "They gotta have you confirm the location of the issue and what needs to be done about it," a man from the corner chimed in. "I know, I know. I just don't know why it had to be me." He let out an uneasy chuckle, and with that, the elevator fell silent once again. I looked back to Sarah. She made a strange face and motioned towards Gary. I gave her an amused smile which she returned.

Sarah was the only woman who voluntarily went underground to check out issues with us. We all respected her for it, but her and I had a special friendship. We had attended the same university and, by chance, ended up working at the same company doing the same job. When a few people from work would go out for happy hour, she would spend most of her time with me, not socializing much with anybody else. Sarah was a flirt, but I never let it get to me- I loved my wife more than anything.

When we reached the bottom, it didn't take too long until we located the problem. A leak in one of the primary pumps was causing the water pressure of the lower east side to decrease exponentially. I walked around the pipes as Gary stood in front of the pump writing things down on a clipboard. Sarah and two other men were investigating the pump up close. The air was thick, and I was beginning to feel uncomfortable.

"You good, Jim?" Sarah asked, looking up at me.

"Yeah, not feeling too hot."

The rest of the group turned their attention to me for a second, stopping their conversation.

"Go grab some water from the backpack over there. This won't take too long," Sarah reminded me kindly.

I smiled and walked over to the backpack leaned up against the wall, grabbing a water bottle from it. My team then resumed their discussion. They were chatting about recent movies that had hit theaters this month. I wasn't too close to hear the full conversation, but I knew one of the men was attempting to sound like a professional critic.

Just then, I could feel a slight rumble beneath my feet. It was very faint and I assumed it was just the pipes since we were in the older part of the city. Only a few seconds later did I feel it again, this time stronger. I looked over to my team, who seemed completely oblivious of what I just felt. The vibrations from the pump must've masked it since they were all huddled near it. I thought for a second if I should bring it to their attention, but I stopped myself. They were having a casual conversation, Gary was much calmer at this point, and I didn't want to seem neurotic. I leaned myself back against the wall and took another sip of water. It wasn't a big deal, I told myself. I had no reason to worry at all, or at least that's what I initially thought.

None of them were prepared when the pipes began to shake rapidly. They looked around in terror as the walls and ceiling began to tremble. Sarah got up from crouching and stumbled back into Gary, knocking the clipboard out of his hands. I should have warned them. Dropping my water to the ground in a panic, I attempted to yell to my team over the loud shaking of the tunnel. Whatever was happening must have triggered a chain reaction in the pipeline causing the leaking pump to burst, catching my team in the explosion. I was knocked back by the sheer force of the blast, and in a dazed state watched as the ceiling began to crack.

I couldn't hear anything over the gushing of water. Water was rising all around me. As my vision became clear again, I could see the crack above me stretching wider. My heart was racing, and after attempting to lift myself back to my feet, I witnessed my team on the ground. My eardrums were ringing and my vision was blurry. I could feel the water rising over my fingers as I pressed my palm against the ground. Looking up, I saw Sarah on the ground, attempting to shake one of the men who was bleeding profusely from his head. His limp body elicited no response. Her leg appeared to be broken, or at least seriously injured. I called out to her, but she couldn't hear me over the now spewing pipe. Water continued to rise. I stumbled forward, the tunnel still shaking violently, and finally grabbed Sarah's attention. She stopped shaking and looked to me. I began to take my first step toward her when the ceiling finally gave in. The faces of my family flashed before my eyes. I stopped and stared at Sarah. She stared back at me. She had pretty eyes.

My body was numb. I felt as if this was my fault. I could've warned them, gotten them away from the pump, away from the blast. I could've done something. The thought of never being able to see my children again stopped me. I could've tried to save her, but I didn't want to die. My kids needed me.

Their bodies were crushed beneath the rubble of the ceiling, and I would soon meet their fate as well if I didn't get the hell out of there. I turned from the heap of cement and metal, frantic and panicking, and began running. The water was still rising, making it increasingly more difficult to trudge through it. The lights began to give out, leaving me in a collapsing labyrinth stranded in darkness. It was then that I realized my phone was still in its bag. Still making my way through the pitch black tunnel, I fumbled around in my pockets and found a lighter. I wasn't a smoker, and luckily for me, I never took the lighter I had used for my son's birthday cake a few days earlier out of my pocket. Navigating the underground maze, I lit my way using the dim flame. My thoughts were on my team. I felt overwhelming guilt. I stared into her eyes as the ceiling came down on her. All because I didn't want to make Gary any more anxious. All because I couldn't leave my children.

The water was up to my knees by the time I reached the incline up to the elevator, and after fiddling with the machine a bit, I realized I'd have to take the ladder. The shaking had stopped at this point, but I still tried to climb the ladder as fast as possible. *Why didn't you say anything, why didn't you try to save her?* I continued to repeat these sentences in my head over and over the whole way up. And hell, it was a long way up.

When I emerged, the city was in obvious disarray. Cars just left in the middle of the street with the doors wide open, bits of rubble scattered about, a few old buildings completely demolished here and there. However, something more strange was the lack of people. Nobody at all. Not even bodies. Calling out yielded no results. The city was silent for the first time.

I was in a state of shock, and found myself just standing there for minutes. I witnessed people die down there- my friends- Sarah. And now there was this. I stumbled over to a car with the door open and the keys still in the ignition. Turning them did nothing. I made my way to the next car in front of it and was met with the same result as the first car. This continued for the next three cars until I realized it couldn't just be coincidence. At this point, I began searching the surrounding buildings. Whether it is a convenience store or a corporate building, none of them had working lights or running power. Whatever happened wiped out any source of electricity and left me stranded here in the middle of a deserted New York City.

I began to think about my family. My whole body was numb again. They were all the way back in Long Island, and I was here without a working car. There had to be a way home, I thought. All my mind could process at that point was getting back to Long Island and back to my family. I frantically tried one last car. The key turned in the ignition and to my dismay shared the same outcome as the other cars. I sat in the driver's seat, turning the key over and over, simply staring out into the field of abandoned cars. Anger overtook my mind, and I began slamming my fists on the dashboard and kicking the gas pedal.

"Goddamnit!" I screamed at the top of my lungs. Removing myself from the car, I began walking.

I didn't care how long it took, but I had to get home. It took me almost a day to travel what usually took under two hours. I passed all sorts of debris, fallen trees and structures, and a sea of abandoned cars along the roads, all of which I assumed to be in an in

operational state based on my previous findings. Some buildings stood while others looked completely decimated, which only furthered my confusion. Scenarios went over and over in my head like clockwork, yet nothing seemed to make sense.

My heart dropped anytime I passed a house with children's' toys in the front yard. My mind would always wander back to my own kids. I needed to know they were safe.

When I finally arrived at my neighborhood, many of the houses were in ruin- completely demolished. I kept praying in my head that my house wasn't like that. I didn't know what I was expecting. My family to be standing right inside like nothing happened?

Well, I didn't get my wish. I stood there, staring at where my house once stood. The place I had come home to for years, always looking forward to walking inside and kneeling down when the kids ran over to me. It was now in shambles. I stood there, just staring. My mind should have had so many thoughts swirling through it, yet it was blank. My home couldn't be gone. *They* couldn't be gone.

I ended up passing out and sleeping in between the rubble of what used to be my house that night after searching hours on end for just a sign of my family. I didn't know if I wanted to find their bodies or not. In a way, if I did I could feel a sense of closure, but nobody wants to see the lifeless bodies of their own children. My search, however, yielded nothing. Not even so much as a photograph. When I awoke, a horrible feeling overtook me when I realized it wasn't all just a bad dream. I felt broken. I sat there all day just lost in my thoughts, not really knowing what to do anymore. I left my neighborhood, my house, my family, and never looked back.

Over the course of the next few weeks, I traveled around in hopes of finding, well, anything. I wasn't sure what I was looking for. Other people or some sort of answer or evidence as to what happened seemed like a good start. Everywhere I went, however, was completely deserted. I wasn't sure if I was isolated from the world, or if the world was isolated from me. I ended up discovering the ham radio and settled down back in New York. It felt like the closest thing to home now. If I was to wait for anybody, it would be there. There were plenty of supplies and shelter, and that's where I spent the next five years- waiting- thinking.

Being alone gives a *lot* of time to think. Time passes much slower without anybody to share it with. Without human contact, I found myself lost in my thoughts all the time. A majority of that thinking was about Jessica and the kids- wherever they were, whatever happened to them. However, most of the time it was memories. Past occurrences that somewhat helped me retain my grip on reality. The familiar sound of Noah and Madison's radiating laughter plagued my thoughts. I would try to remember back to my old life just to hear their voices again, as it was the only way now.

"What happened, honey? Why are you all dirty?" I asked a dirt-covered Madison as she slumped inside, attempting to finish folding a shirt from the laundry basket so I could tend to her.

"Noah's being a meanie. He threw dirt at me, can you go yell at him?" I tossed the shirt onto the bed; the pressure put on me from Madison wasn't helping my already lackluster folding performance.

"Here, let's go get you cleaned up, then we'll talk to Noah." She trailed me to the bathroom, sat up on the toilet, all the while watching as I grabbed a washcloth. After I ran the towel beneath some running water, I kneeled down and began dabbing it on Madison's face. "I didn't get to ask you about school this week, how'd it go? Anything exciting happen?"

She stared at me for a second before responding with a quick, "I don't remember." I paused for a second and gave her a face of curiosity, which she must have found silly because I saw that big radiant smile that I loved so much, followed by a bit of giggling. "Uh, oh I remember this one thing. We had show and tell and I brought Cera."

"Which dinosaur is Cera again?"

She looked slightly concerned, as if this was information I should have 100% known.

"The triceratops, daddy!" Madison exclaimed.

Duh, I thought to myself, *that was her favorite one.*

"Didn't you already bring her to show and tell?" I asked. "Yeah, I wanted to bring Bodie but mommy said no." She pouted.

I had just finished cleaning the dirt off of her, picked her up, and began heading towards the backyard.

"Bodie needs to stay home, sweets. He's a living animal."

"That's what mommy said, too!"

We got the kids a hamster after years of them begging for a dog. Jessica and I felt for the kids, but the simple fact that Jessica was extremely allergic to dogs held us back. We ended up surprising them with a hamster, and the rest is history. Noah was excited at first, but his interest in the small creature withered over the course of maybe a week. On the other hand, Madison loved it to death. She was responsible for his name, Bodie, playing with him, and everything in between. Jessica took care of feeding and cleaning his cage, but was slowly teaching Madison. Noah still wanted a dog.

I could hear the faint laughter as I made my way to the glass sliding door off the living room. It was open a crack from when Madison slumped inside, the small trail of dirt was evidence enough of this. She continued to talk about the events that unfolded at show and tell, and with the combined efforts of Madison's voice next to my ear, Noah's giggling from outside, and my own thoughts focused on how I would get the stains out of the carpet before my wife got home, my mind zoned itself out and took everything in as one. It was just noise to me, and if

I realized how important those sounds were at the time, I would have cherished every moment.

The human mind is wondrous and complex, but it's also very evil. As my thoughts degraded into loose hallucinations and jumbled messes, my memories remained, almost as if my mind was taunting me. Most of the time, I didn't care. I was just glad I could vaguely remember a time when I was happy. A time when I wasn't alone.

I leaned over the concrete precipice, looking over the city. A slight breeze ruffled through my hair. It had been a normal day. A normal day consisting of trudging through the same rut I had been in for half a decade. I made my way back to the radio, slumped down in my chair, and threw back another gulp of whisky. I could feel the effects of the alcohol in full force. It seemed ironic that I finally had straight-forward thoughts once I felt intoxicated. Maybe not coherent thoughts, but thoughts nonetheless. It wasn't the same mindset I'd had for a while now. My usual blank mind was filled with thoughts, memories, and questions. *Why I am still here? What's keeping me from just ending it all? I have nobody. No friends, no family. No purpose anymore. There's no point to this everyday struggle.*

I thought back to the hallucinations I had this morning. A few people gathered at the corner of 5th and 23rd. Just standing in a circle, talking, with smiles on their faces. They were joking about something, but their voices were incoherent. The memory was fuzzy. When I tried to approach them, they turned and scoffed. I felt light headed for a second and the street corner returned to its usual desolate state. The hallucinations, in a way, were a blessing and a curse. For a split few seconds, I didn't feel alone anymore. There were things happening that broke up the monotony of the real world, but more importantly, there were people. I could feel a little less alone for those few seconds where my subconscious, in its obvious ill state, projected what I guess I desired most into the world. Soon after, however, they would disappear, giving me the grim reminder once more that I was it- the only one.

The alcohol reminded me of the nights I'd stay up with my friends, busting each other's stones about our fantasy football league sitting around my basement table, of the small get-together's with the family on the holidays, of the happy hour outings I would attend with my co-workers every other Friday afternoon- with Sarah. I thought back to her eyes, and the fear she had in them. It felt like my fault.

My family was home that day. It was a missed opportunity. Yet, I couldn't miss one measly day of work. It was always work, work, work. If I stayed with them, something might've been different. Even still, if everything turned out the same, I could be with them... *with them.* Why wasn't I with them?

I quaffed down rest of the bottle and threw it at the ground in a drunken rage, tears streaming down my cheek. I flipped the table with the radio still on it, still droning on. It slammed to the ground, a few pieces of plastic chipped off and were scattered across the rooftop. I turned and kicked the chair, my pistol flying off and landing next to my foot. Staring down at it, I had made my choice. I was alone for too long. Looking back to the broken shards of glass, a sense of purpose overtook me. After everything I had been through, this was the catalyst. A simple bottle of booze. This was it. I leaned down and picked up the gun.

I had given up. I didn't know why I kept going. Maybe it was a side effect of my self-diagnosed insanity. Or maybe it was something more. But it was gone now. I didn't know if everyone else was dead, or if I was, but at this point it didn't matter. Anything is better than this. Lying there, I tried to think about my family- my children, their faces. I closed my eyes, and there they were. Two faces, smiling at me. I don't even know if my children looked like that, but I didn't care. I wanted them to be their faces, so they were. Their comforting words soothed me as I pointed the gun towards my mouth. The static of the radio droned on and held my thoughts together. Their bright faces, how joyful they looked, telling me it would be okay. I finally felt happy again. I laid my finger on the trigger.

And just like that, the ham radio's monotone static muffled, and faint voice could be heard from the other side. I could only make out one thing: "Can you hear me?"

Yes. Yes, I can hear you.

Ten and One

"M"orning Reggie, how's that shoulder," I said making my way past the metal detectors at the building entrance.

"Morning, Maya- it's been better," he said with a slight smile.

"The boss has another big one for you today," he continued, waving his metal detector around as if he was an extra in Star Wars.

"That's great but watch where you're waving that thing Reg," I said, laughing and ducking a few of his swings.

Jogging up the large spiral staircase to my office, I rushed inside before the boss could see me. He was a talker and I had actually wanted to get some work done today. I turned on my desk lamp and put in my headphones before opening the file that had been left on my desk. Flipping furiously through the pages I was in a slight disbelief, I was staring down my first murder case. If having a ten case win streak didn't help my credibility, winning a case like this would certainly help. My eyes skimmed the front page of the packet. *Alex Lowry, 26 years old, second-degree murder.*

Vaguely, I remembered hearing his name on the news a few nights back while mindlessly flipping through channels. His situation was something I had initially shrugged off, another rich kid in a mess. I scanned a few of the lines from the police reports the boss had printed out for me, laying out the details of the incident and the defendant's arrest.

"Victim found dead in locker room showers with what appears to be a fractured skull. Main suspect brought in from crime scene," I read aloud

159

to myself, my eyes rolled down the page searching for any information that would help me later on. Alex had been released on bail the next day, returning to campus as if nothing ever happened. It was even listed that he attempted to practice with the team before being escorted out of the gym.

A quick burst of knocks on my office door shook me to my core, awakening me from my trance like state of concentration and nearly spooking me out of my skin.

"Come in," I answered quickly, watching Nina, the office secretary enter with what I assumed was the Lowry family.

They entered my office quickly and quietly, backs hunched and heads bowed. Alex's mother had clearly been crying before entering the room. Her cheeks were red with faded streaks of black and blotchy makeup that looked as if they had splattered in carelessly. There was nothing a jury would sympathize with more than a grieving mother on the brink of losing her only child. The only thing that could give our case a better edge would be getting his father to cry too.

"This is the Lowry family. Let me know if you need anything else, Maya" she said with a smile before turning and shutting the door.

"Hello, I'm Maya Miller, you can call me Maya," I said, extending my hand forward.

"I'm Richard, this is my wife Helen and I assume you know our son, Alex," he trailed off. I nodded letting a slight smile roll across my face.

"Do you know what you're doing, I don't mean to sound so blunt I just…..My family….you better know what you're doing," the mother spoke up and my eyes widened a bit. Her words were sharp and cold, hitting me like a strong gust of wind.

"I assure you, ma'am, I will do everything I can to help your family. As long as Alex is transparent and honest with me you all will receive the best results possible," I replied. She dipped her head solemnly, turning toward Alex whose presence was almost ghostly.

"Can you do that for me Alex?" I asked, trying to force some sort of response.

His father nudged his shoulder causing him to sit upright in his seat. Leaning his head back against the wall, Alex finally gave me a good look at his face. His eyes laid dark, almost sunken into his skull, while his arms hung down by his side.

"Anything you want to add, Alex," I said in an effort to draw some sort of reaction. He shrugged, still staring at the ceiling I leaned forward in my chair and watched Alex for a few seconds.

"The only way this works is if you put in as much effort into this as I will Alex," I started. He bowed his head quickly making brief eye contact.

"Let's get to work. You're the basketball teams captain, correct?"

"Actually, not in front of them.....If we're going to do this, they need to go," he responded. *So he does speak* . I stared intently at the desk before making my next move. Shining an apologetic smile at his parents I stood up making my way toward the door.

"We aren't going anywhere, anything he can say to a stranger he can certainly say in front of us," Alex's father asserted. I opened my office door and stood in the frame,

"Mr. Lowry, I understand your concern for your son but he is the one I am defending. As much as I would like to turn this into a group therapy session, I think our time would be put to better use if we all did whatever we could to make this run smoothly," I started, making eye contact with all three members of the Lowry clan. Mr.Lowry's scowl quickly became a frown.

"If you have any questions later on I'd be happy to answer the, but right now, i'd really like to help your son." Mrs.Lowry grabbed her husband's hand and looked up at him with sad eyes before standing herself.

"Call us if you need anything Alex," his mother called as they made their way out.

"Before we star......"

"Are you going to get me off or what?" He interrupted.

"That is.....my job in a sense," I answered, taking note of Alex's new found confidence.

"Then lets get this over with, I've got places to be?" He replied with a blank stare. I was slightly disappointed the heat from my stare didn't burn a hole in the front of his head. My frustration was getting the best of me as I bit my tongue hard enough to draw blood.

"Would one of these places happen to be the state prison?" I quipped.

"Excuse me?" Alex muttered. I could tell he wasn't used to being challenged.

"That's where you'll end up if you can't take this seriously, and that won't be my fault. It will be yours," I finished, watching Alex shrink back down into his seat.

Not wanting to waste any more time, I made an effort to move the meeting along. I had known a few of the minor details. Alex was the perfect specimen. A business student at the Northwestern University, Starting Point guard and debate team captain. On top of this, coming from a well-connected and wealthy family clearly hadn't made him the most humble. It was no surprise he had expected some sort of special treatment.

I opened the blinds, letting in some natural light and waited for Alex to begin his story. His presence became less ghastly when the light filled the room. Moving back toward my desk I sat and opened my laptop and opened a new file for Alex. Looking up at Alex, I gave him a nod as if to tell him to begin.

"I went back to the lockers after practice to clean up, it was the beginning of the season so the whole team was in- it was our first practice"

"That's where Steven died- the locker room?" my eyes fell to him, trying to connect with his, hoping to see what was going through Alex's head.

"Yes… In the team's defense, that's never happened before. That's what we do with the freshmen, that's how you keep them in line" Alex sat back in his chair crossing his arms and legs.

"What do you mean by 'that's never happened before'?" I asked.

"We play the same prank every year, it's kind of a tradition. The freshmen have to run through the showers fully clothed, waters scalding hot you should see it it's actually pretty funny," he laughed and looked up to see if I had found it funny as well. "I had to do it my freshman year and it wasn't so bad," he added and looked up at me to see if my expression had changed.

"Anyways yeah one kid took a few steps backward, slipped and hit his head on the shower handle," he said nonchalantly before leaning back in his seat and letting out a silent yawn.

"Well this is obviously quite the tragedy, you lost teammate and a friend. Are you experiencing any guilt?" I asked, watching Alex in an attempt to gage his emotions.

"Not really. It sucks that he died but that wasn't really my fault."

I could feel the veins popping up in my forehead as he spoke.

"Never say that again, to me or anyone else. For the next few weeks we are going to work on your testimony and defense. You will show up to every meeting and court date on time. Dress up, keep it dark and simple. Your only job is to appeal to the Jury's emotions. Write down everything you knew about Steven. Hobbies, favorite color, favorite food and study it. We'll get into more detail tomorrow."

After Alex left, I stayed behind another hour or so writing out my game plan for the next day. We had a lot to go over and this kid was piece of work. I locked up my office and began to head out.

"You need a hand, Reg?" I asked, watching as he struggled to carry what looked like trash bags through the large blue glass doors. Before he could answer I grabbed the bags from him and tossed them in the dumpster around the side of the building. We exchanged smiles and walked back toward the firm's entrance. I watched as Nina made her way out of the doors, emerging looking very frazzled and stressed.

"How did I finish my work before you? Must've had a lot of copies to make." I laughed.

"Yeah, yeah, I know. I had some last-minute studying to do, sorry," she replied. I watched as as a mountain of criminal law books and re-search papers landed callously in the back seat.

"Practice tests giving you trouble?" I asked, motioning to the books.

"Trouble is and understatement. I don't know what's worse, failing the BAR the first time or deciding to or actually taking it again," she responded.

"You're going to do fine this time. You've got nothing to worry about," I said sliding into the driver's seat.

"I hear your new case is a big one, hook me up with the details c'mon," Nina started I causing me to roll my eyes and laugh.

"Eh, some jerk kid being charged with murder," I said trying to hide my excitement.

"You think he did it?," She said with her eyes wide.

"I have no idea. It honestly feels like it could go either way," I responded. The rest of the car ride home was about anything we could think of that wasn't work related. We got inside and I plopped down into my sweet spot, where I did all my best work.

"You really need to clean that space up. How old are you, seven?" Nina called from the kitchen.

"This is where the magic happens bud, rearranging things would only mess up my flow" I laughed.. It was crunch time. Time to focus on the case. Alex's story had seemed true enough. No details seemes to be out of place and we could easily win the jury over if we played our cards right. I still needed a lot more information. To build a proper defense I searched for anything that might incriminate Alex.

"Let's run through this one more time. Why do people think you did this, why are they trying to charge with the murder of Steven?" I asked, moving in a little closer. He looked at me with squinted eyes and shrugged.

"How should I know? Unless they know something I don't I'm innocent," he said with a little fire in his voice.

"Of course you know. You're the team captain, a leader. You've lead your team in, and participated in hazing for years, which you have just admitted to," he gave me a sharp look and repositioned himself in his seat. "You're facing class four felony charges- one to six years in prison."

I'd be lying to myself if I said I wasn't trying to scare him a little. It was a technique that often worked. My goal was to see if his story would change, how shaken up he might be. I purposefully left out the maximum $25,000 fine, if anything that would provide him with a sense of comfort. Money was no object to the Lowry's and that was less than they were paying me.

"It's not really hazing we just…. We were just team bonding, you know?" he fumbled over his words and I watched as his face grew cherry red. Guilty or not, Alex was a complete nervous wreck.

I threw my sheet of questions across the room onto my desk and watched as it landed, knocking down a few stacks on its way over. I let out a heavy sigh while making my way over to the seat next to Alex and clapped for his attention.

"Let's go over this again, Alex. You need to answer confidently. I'm going to hit you with everything I've got so think this stuff through."

His eyes glazed over the question cheat sheet I had typed up earlier. I had hoped giving him some idea of how I would answer the questions would help him to answer them better. He nodded and wiped the sweat that had started to bead on his forehead.

"Why was Steven...," I paused and watched as his eyes grew glossy and red. He brought his hands to his face and covered his eyes while taking a deep breath. A single tear managed to escape his cupped hands.

"Why was Steven fully dressed in formal attire when the police arrived?" I continued in an effort to push him. He needed to pull it together.

"You can't cry on the stand Alex. To some it shows sympathy but to others it admits guilt. It's best to keep your emotions neutral. Now, answer the question."

I shoved my hands into my pockets and waited for his response.

"The incoming freshmen do it every year. I did it, the class before me did it. It's just tradition" He answered, not raising his face from his hands.

I watched him for a second before walking toward my desk. Alex needed to calm down if he was going to have any real shot at swaying the jury in his direction.

"I think that will be all for today Alex, go home and get some rest alright?" Alex nodded, rising slowly from his seat and making his way towards my office door.

Searching up the Northwestern Basketball coach was last on my to do list. Giving him a call I sat and listened to the monotonous ring of the phone. I asked him a few questions about Alex in regards to how he treated his team and if there was anyone he had problems with, especially Steven. Apparently, Alex was no longer starting point guard. The victim, Steven, had been recently bumped into his position. His hatred for Steven didn't have much to do with the hazing, especially since other boys were victims as well, but at least now I could prepare a defense for this new information. I told him to have any of the other players contact me if they had anything they could add.

After a few days of running through the court process with Alex, I received an email. Anonymous, but I had assumed it was from one of the players. I opened it, expecting more minor details about Alex as a captain and a teammate. Reading through the email thoroughly, I made sure not to miss any information that might be helpful to Alex's case. Nothing seemed to stand out to me initially, but, a video clip that had been attached to the message. It wasn't just a video- it was the video, the hazing in the locker room, clearly depicting Alex tripping the young man who had unknowingly made himself an enemy to him. Underneath was an audio clip. Alex drunkenly explaining his hatred for the poor kid- how he didn't belong on the team and wasn't worthy of the starter position. I rested my head on my desk and thought of all the ways both of those things combined would affect not on the jury's decisions but Alex's sentencing. Underneath the two pieces of evidence were the words *Do the right thing.* To others, the right thing would be to continue on with my case as if nothing had ever happened. I was torn. I had a perfect win record. 5-0 on my major cases so far. Morally I had a duty to turn him in. If he had told me the truth I would only be able to continue on with the case. On the other hand, I promised I would help. Court was the next day and I had to make a decision quick.

"Why are you still up?" called Nina from the kitchen. I hadn't even realized it was three o'clock in the morning but it hadn't mattered much either way.

"Finishing touches," I replied, rubbing my face in frustration. I had a big decision to make and there was no easy way to make it. Nina walked over toward my sweet spot, stumbling over a few books on the way, and handed me a glass of water.

"I swear if you don't clean this up I will. Sweet is the last word I would use to describe this mess," she laughed pushing a stack of papers aside with her foot. Shaking my head, I motioned for her to go back to bed so I could finish my work. I typed up an email for the judge, not sure if I was going to press send. Feeling my perfect case win record slipping away from me, I struggled to to even get the first few words down. Each line seemed more painful to type than the last, however, this seemed to be the right thing to do. I added the video clip to the end of the email, in hopes that seeing the finished product would make me more willing to send it.

I left my laptop open, with an email designated for the judge. In it were the video and sound clip. My heart raced as my finger hovered over the send button but I couldn't make myself do it. I wasn't sure of what to do with it. I slept on my decision and made my way to the courtroom the next morning, where I met Alex and his parents. All three looked as if they had been crying. I had only noticed the puffiness and red tint in Alex' eyes when he had removed his sunglasses upon entering the courtroom.

"All rise for the honorable Judge Henley," spoke the tall officer standing in front of the courtroom.

My decision had to be made and it had to be made quickly. Alex was guilty, I knew that, not only of hazing but of the purposeful assault of Steven, resulting in his death. The video depicted it clear as day. I had told Alex he couldn't cry in the courtroom but now I was wanting to. My hands stuck to the handles of my brief case, they were growing more clammy by the second. I had two options, I could bring the case home, lessen Alex's sentence, maybe even get him to walk, or I could throw this case. Open with a weak statement, ask counterproductive questions. Neither of the options had been too good. I told him I wasn't the judge, but I also knew he hadn't deserved to be a free man.

"Miss Miller…. Your statement please" I snapped back to reality, noticing the curious eyes that had been staring at me. I hopped to my feet making my way to the front of the courtroom. Before I could speak, the Judge's secretary made her way into the courtroom, they shared whispers and strange looks. The judge stood to her feet and Called for a short recess. I know what this means. I just don't know how. I didn't…… oh god. I made my way out to the lobby and reached for my phone that had vibrated, interrupting my panic. Nina: "Really gotta clean that "sweet spot" of yours <3".

A New Beginning to a Tragic Ending

C losing time!" yelled Jane across the maze of wooden tables that rocked on the old uneven diner floor. I creaked across the hardwood floors and locked the front door, gently tossing the "closed" sign across the window. The sound of the change from our small income being counted behind me. If we didn't get our act together, we would miss this old place. I jumped up as I heard a glass rattling shriek come from the cash register. Looking up, I saw Jane's horrified face staring at the register.

"Bradley... we're 100 dollars short today," Jane lightly whispered as so Jon wouldn't hear.

We needed that 100 dollars. The diner was failing and we already had Jon, the penny-pinching owner, breathing down our necks. He had told us stories of when his father owned the business and the fun he had working there as a young kid. He was only 20 and had no idea how to run the business. He had wanted to be a police officer in town but after his dad passing, he couldn't let go of the place.

It was hot here in Cedar Creek as I walked back to my small house where I resided with my mom and grandma. I opened the door and a gust of cold air conditioning hit me, as I felt a relief from the harsh Texas heat. 'Gramma' was propped in her rocking chair stitching together a quilt out of some old shirts she picked up at the local consignment shop. I tried to pitch in all I could from my pay, but with the diner failing, I haven't gotten many tips. Usually I would use my tips to help out with bills, but times were changing. We sat around our small round table and chatted around our dinner. I had brought home the leftover meatloaf from the diner. It was Gramma's favorite. She loved having ketchup with her food. I was more of a gravy person. Gramma coughed into her napkin rather roughly. It sounded very chilling.

"Gramma are you okay?", I asked.

"Perfectly fine dear", she responded as she smiled back at me.

I saw her hiding red in her napkin as she crumpled it up.

"Gramma are you bleeding? I prodded.

"Oh this?" she asked as she waved her napkin. "This is just ketchup from the meatloaf" She responded with an uncomfortable chuckle.

The rest of dinner proceeded normally with Mom asking me questions about work, and Gramma gazing at me, admiring me. I really wasn't much to admire. I graduated high school last year and got caught up with helping mom pay bills, and work at the diner. Although I didn't have many plans yet, my grandma always looked at me admiringly. Dinner ended and I headed upstairs to write in my journal. I used to think journaling was petty, but when Dad died, it helped me vent. Going to a shrink was too expensive, and I couldn't talk to Mom because she was a wreck already.

My dad had died less than a year ago. Although time has passed, my family's wounds were nowhere near mended. He was the financial rock to our family, working as an IT technician, making almost six figures. He never thought to get life insurance, so when he died we were left with nothing.

Work is getting worse… we were short 100 dollars, leaving us with the possibility of not having jobs. Jon didn't want to say the restaurant was soon to close, but we all knew it would. That 100 dollars was needed just to keep the lights on.

I need the pay. We are living paycheck to paycheck, and all the food we eat is leftovers from the diner. What would we do without the diner money?

We need to figure out a plan.

I miss Dad.

I wrote these thoughts down in my journal. Closed the curtain, and drifted off to bed.

I woke up to the sound of my Mom screaming. She never screamed. I heard the urgency in her voice and ran to her. She was on the ground with my grandma, who appeared to look unconscious. I was too frightened to ask what had happened. I saw a small stream of blood coming from out of her mouth, and then I remembered that spot of ketchup on her napkin from last night. Could it have been blood? I just ran to the phone and dialed 911.

After waiting in the hospital, Doctor Williams came out, reporting to us that my Gramma had passed out. They weren't exactly sure what was the cause, but they figured it would be best to keep her overnight for observation. I began to recall the rough coughing that Gramma had, maybe that had something to do with her passing out. "They'll figure it out honey." My mom reassured me. It was 10 am, and the diner was set to open at 11. Mom dropped me off on the way home. She waved out the window to Jon, who gave her a smug nod of his head, as if he didn't care to say hello, yet didn't want to be rude. Jon was my boss, yes the man who was about to yell at me for being short 100 dollars yesterday. Walking up to him, he greeted me saying

"I'm so glad you're here".

This was a pleasant surprise, but I was taken back because I wasn't being reprimanded for losing the money.

"Is everything okay?" I asked him in a sarcastic manner.

"Hey I can be nice sometimes can't I?" He jokingly responded.

"Sureeeeeeee" I said, letting out small giggles as we walked up to the door.

"Let's go inside, I have important news to discuss with you." Jon said to me.

He sounded almost happy, so I basically bounced with excitement as I followed him. Maybe the restaurant wasn't failing after all. We walked in and I saw Jane in the first booth on the left. I saw her quickly wipe a tear with her long white blouse. Jon and I joined Jane at the booth, where we continued our conversation from outside.

"Bradley, I'm closing the diner by the end of the week. The bills are adding up, the customers aren't coming, and we aren't making enough profit to keep the doors open."

Not sure what to say, I just stared at the etchings in our old wooden tables. The etchings showed signs of happy customers that once enjoyed the diner, as me and my family did when I was younger. My shift started, only serving one party for the first few hours we were open. Everything was going good until a young boy dropped his ice water on my beat up, hole filled, shoes. Ignoring the freezing temperatures that my toes endured, I continued my shift. At 10 o'clock I grabbed some food and began the short walk back home.

Walking down the street, I could hear sirens roaring down the road. They were going towards my house. A slight thought in the back of my head made me believe it could be an emergency at my house, so I began to jog. As I neared my house, I saw two medics loading a stretcher through my front door. At this point, I was frantic. I pushed through the fields of medics, and found my mom sitting at the table.

"It's your grandma. She passed out like last time, but she had been coughing up blood beforehand."

Not knowing what to say, I sat down and held my mother's hand. Mom was short of words, which was shocking, especially when it had to do with something as expensive as an ambulance ride. We soon got up and stood by my Gramma's side as she was wheeled off to the ambulance. We trailed behind the screaming ambulance in my mom's old beat up wagon, as I wondered what they were doing to Gramma.

Was she safe? Was she unconscious? What was happening?

We arrive at the hospital where we encountered a snooty young girl at the front desk asking us to sign in.

"My grandma was just brought in on a stretcher." I asked urgently.

"Okay well you're just going to have to sign in right here," she said, pointing to a clipboard on the hard desk.

Where is my mother?" my Mom yelled at the now scared girl.

She pointed towards the ER down the hall.

We stood by the large doors that lead to the ER, watching through the small glass windows as the doctors brought a crash cart to my Gramma's side. They began to shock her with the defibrillator, but after multiple times, my Gramma wasn't waking up.

Why wasn't she waking up? What had happened during that time when I was at work?

The doctor had literally just sent her home a few hours ago after being observed. I screamed all of these questions in a panic as I leaned on my mom, who was speechless. I saw the sad looks on the doctor's faces as they covered Gramma's lifeless face with the white sheet. My mother was sobbing as two nurses pulled us away from our front row seats at the ER doors. A young, tall skinny doctor with a distraught face came out and approach my mother and I.

"Despite our efforts," he began to say.

"I already know what you're going to say", my Mom began to quiver. "Just stop! Please," she pleaded.

The sad look on the doctor's face made me realize that my Gramma had actually died. "I'm so sorry for your loss", he said as he put his head down and walked out the doors. After filling out paperwork, my mom and I left the hospital around 1 am, where we proceeded to stop at the local diner to try and get some food in our nauseous bodies. We really only wanted to get away from the painful thoughts of my Gramma being gone.

The days went on as my mother and I mourned the loss of my Gramma. Tomorrow was the funeral, something we were both not looking forward to. We both couldn't believe that Gramma never told us about having lung cancer. Perhaps it was because she knew we couldn't afford the treatment. I went outside to check the mail, but the harsh morning sun stopped me in my tracks. I wasn't used to the harsh heat, as my mom and I spent our days following my grandma's death, inside the house. I opened the mailbox and only found one letter. It was addressed to my mother, and had an important notice saying "Payment inside, do not discard". I brought the check to my mom and she sighed.

"This is a blessing in disguise she told me" as she opened letter, finding a hundred thousand dollar check inside.

My mom explained to me that this was from my Gramma's life insurance. I guess my father hadn't been wise enough to pay for his own life insurance, but he did for my Gramma. My Gramma had made most of the income to keep our family afloat, so insurance reimbursed us a good sum of cash. We sat at the table and cried, as we wished we could replace the 100,000 dollars with my Gramma.

The day after the funeral, my mom and I headed down to the diner, where Jon was taking down signs, preparing to evict the building. We approached him and told him we'd like to buy the business from him. He was shocked but ecstatic. My mom proceeded to discuss our finances with him, but they soon agreed on a fair buying price. I was eager, because my Gramma would live on in this restaurant. My mom and I would run the business and be able to support ourselves. This was a new beginning, for us. We signed some papers with Jon, who had called his lawyer and had him come down immediately. We were told that once the check goes through, the restaurant was all ours. I couldn't believe this was happening. I realized this was a gamble, as the diner could fail. But Jane and I knew the business; we would just have to teach my mom. As soon as the diner was ours, my mom and I decided we would change the name. I went down to the hardware store and bought plywood and paint. I then proceeded to design the restaurant's new sign. My mom stood over me, rubbing my shoulder as she approved of the name. Next week, Gramma's Diner would be open for business.

A Drink to Last a Lifetime

Ma'am, we have a few questions to ask you regarding the incident that took place earlier," the police officer said for the third time.

"Now isn't a good time," I said, my body pressed up against the door, enabling me to see the cops through the eyehole.

"Ma'am it would be easier if you would cooperate and open up," the cop's voice got louder. The silence was growing as was the length of his breathing, in through his nose and out through the mouth.

"I have to do a few things right now. Just come back later and we can talk."

"My partner and I will be back in two hours, and expect to talk," the cop's voice withered away in the air as they were leaving.

Walking away, the officers' cologne drifted under the door, the scent finding its way up into my lungs. The intense scent turned my stomach into knots and sent me into the bathroom hurling my head over the toilet. Wiping the drool off of my chin, I took a sip of some drink left out from the night before to wash my mouth.

I only knew Stanley from a distance Although he was my neighbor, I barely knew anything about the man. He hated me and I hated me so we had that in common. The way he moaned at the 2 A.M. noise I would make when stumbling up the stairs to my apartment dropping an empty bottle on the ground, I could tell he wasn't a fan from the start. The glass would cover the hallway and make it smell like cheap liquor. He would never fail to shout out an insult; like a disappointed father would say to his daughter when he finds out that she just happened to be at a party where people were drinking. In the moment I just found it funny.

I could use a drink right about now, my watch says 11:15 A.M. but it's five o'clock somewhere. Everything is a fog, my head is still pounding from last night; I could barely see straight. I carefully opened the fridge in hopes to find something edible, but with only two beers and leftovers from last week, my stomach only curled more. The thought of the cops coming over meant that I had to clean up. I had about two minutes to make the place look like no one lived here.

I won't drink right now. There is no need to drink right now, Emily. You have company coming over. You need to clean up. The pep talk gave me the motivation to do something, but not enough to clean at that moment. The empty apartment next door intrigued me and with just enough curiosity and beer in me, I had to venture in, just to see how he was living. I could only imagine the trash piled up to the ceiling, like something out of the show Hoarders.

Waiting for Stanley's voice to reappear, I stood outside to see if I could still hear him nagging me to get my life together. There were no broken bottles on the floor today only muddy tracks from the cops' shoes. The door shut behind me abruptly, making my body shake even more. With hesitation, I walked over to Stanley's now vacant apartment. Making my way in the door, it felt desolate, in my head I can picture an opera room without an audience but a woman was still singing, with a single tear trailing down her cheek.

Falling off the door by the careless touch of the cops, the caution tape floated from the draft of the heater and draped onto the floor. I found my hand touching the doorknob and my head filling with distant memories. A few months ago, Stanley was walking up the stairs, chatting with someone. Not until looking out my door, when I saw no one with him is when I started to think he was at his wit's end.

I barely remembered what happened last night, or even in the last few hours. Turning the knob slowly, I pushed the wooden door in as it let out a loud creak, making my ears ring like an alarm. The mid-January cold bursts of wind got into the apartment and started to flood the place as if it was a freezer. Dancing to the rhythm of the wind, the curtains drifted in the breeze. The sun beamed across the floor lighting up only half of the room. Though the sun was glistening in and the lights were on, it still felt cold. I did a spin around to see if anything looked out of the ordinary. I have never been inside of Stanley's apartment, but somehow that didn't bother me. What bothers me is how empty the apartment was. Scattered across the floor, were papers and trinkets. Against the walls, along the floorboards, books were lined up next to each other, their bindings touching one another. The cobwebs on the books seemed to be undisturbed, so naturally I had to be the one to touch everything. In the kitchen, a small window light appeared and directly shined onto a single book. The light caught the pages frozen by the intricate spider webs and dust collected for months. It caught the corner of my eye. Stumbling along, I crouched down to look at it. As I picked the book up, a small spider darted from the bottom of it. His shelter for the night was destroyed but his cobwebs still remained on the book. With a swift swipe on the cover to get the dust, a name appeared, Stanley E. Whitmore. An echo throughout the apartment rang, it kept the hair on my body standing up as my knee gave out falling to the ground.

I guess I could sit down, but only for a few minutes. As I opened the book, the smell overcame me. It brought me back to when I was little and how the books at the used book corner store smelt just like it. It was clear that this book hasn't been touched in some time. That didn't stop me from reading. It has never stopped me; not even when my mother was throwing the older books in the library down and making me look for something younger and newer.

Dropping the book onto the ground, let it open by itself and have me at no fault for opening it, truly an accident. The handwritten paragraphs on the pages are no novel. The book wasn't a novel, or even a New York Times bestseller- it was his journal. I don't know Stanley that well. A peek into someone else's world is a lot better than tripping over yourself in your dimmed lit apartment.

Trickling my fingers down the spine of the book, I knew deep down underneath the thick coating of alcohol that touching his journals could possibly be a bad decision. Then again a possible bad consequence has never stopped me. I could vouch and say that our encounters in the hall-way and conversations that include yelling at 2 A.M. would constitute as me knowing him. My nosey self took-over and I began to read to myself.

179

December 19th, 1954

I know it has been awhile since I have updated this, but I should have you know that my dear Elizabeth is pregnant. I haven't been this excited since my father got me a Schwinn New World bike for my 10th birthday. I can still feel my hair flowing in the wind as I ride down the hill over on Clover Street. Hours on end I would ride that thing, without a care in the world. I would explore every part of the town- seeing "what America has to offer." I guess that feeling never drifted away. Now I can share that experience with Elizabeth and our child. I'm going to be a father. A dad. I am still in shock. A daughter too. Some guys would be mad that they won't have a son to play catch with or go see a baseball game with. Me? I am happy to have even been blessed to have a child. A girl too. She'll be just like Elizabeth. Though the doctors aren't 100% sure that we are having a girl, they don't want to get our hopes up. Old wives tales have told us that we are having a girl; Elizabeth was so sick during the first few months; people tell us that since her morning sickness was god awful, she's having a girl. Elizabeth has a few names in mind, I quite like-

The rest of the entry was torn out, it was illegible.

With the encounters of Stanley Whitmore and I being few and far between, I never thought he was a husband, let alone a father. I always thought he was some sad old man who never got married. Stanley never had anyone over, at least he never did when I was awake.

Standing up, I shoved the book underneath my arm as I began looking around the apartment-maybe there was something-anything-that could show me who he was, who he had been. Looking around the apartment, his kitchen caught my eye. Sitting in the basin, a few utensils and plates sat soaking in water. Above it, the cabinets stood, all torn open, nakedly bare of any contents-as if their only purpose was to house more cobwebs, just as his journal had done. Despite any noticeable food, the smell that came from inside the cupboard made my headache grow worse.

As soon as I stepped in his room, I could feel him. The bed was well kept, neatly folded and made to perfection. Three bookcases were filled with all different books, from Hemingway to Stephen King. Some clothes were scattered on the floor. Drawers were open, like someone had ransacked the place.

Looking at my watch to see when the cops are coming, hairs start to stand up as I realize an hour and a half have passed. Dropping every thought of Stanley to rush around and get ready, I make sure that everything is in a place or at least in a closet pushing against each other. Opening my door to a ransacked apartment that I created, made my heart race. Knowing that people were coming over, I tried to hide as much of the clutter that would fit in out of sight cabinets.

The smell of alcohol overcame me and my clothes. Searching for mouthwash, I tried to clean out any trace of alcohol. Whooshing around the mouthwash in and around my teeth, the buzzer chimed. A smiled dawned upon my face as I rang them up. Looking at myself in the mirror I can feel a sense of comfort knowing someone other than myself, a random cat, and a few week old pizza boxes are in my apartment.

A strong knock rang throughout the entire desolate apartment, making the empty cans shake. The cops' feet were making more noise than the tv in the back room. Pulling out chairs, the two of them sat down.

"Hello ma'am, I'm detective Coffman and this is my partner, Danny. We came to talk to you about the events occurring earlier involving Stanley Whitmore, your neighbor. We just need a few minutes of your time," The cop's breath smelt like day-old coffee.

Trying to keep whatever I had in my stomach down, I said, "Yeah sure I don't remember much but here have a seat," I lead them into the kitchen pulling out chairs for them.

"Sit down I have all day to talk."

"This will only take a few minutes. So at 4:50 this morning we received an alert from Stanley's call monitor indicating a 911 call. When we arrived on scene you were outside of your apartment on the ground, looking like you were passed out. When we entered Mr. Whitmore's apartment we found him on the ground, face down. At this point, you stumbled in murmuring words. We just wanted to know if you happen to see anyone go into Stanley's apartment or if you went in there. If you didn't see anyone come in or out maybe heard something?" The cop simply stating facts that everyone already knew seemed like he couldn't care less. His eyes wandering all over my apartment, making slight judgments about every knick-knack I had laying around.

"No, I don't remember ever stumbling into his apartment when you were there and I certainly don't remember if I heard or saw anything."

Red in the face and a racing heartbeat grew my rage with the irresponsible fact that they still don't understand I can barely remember if I threw out the bottles with moldy oranges in them.

"Emily is it, I think you do remember, and I just think you are too drunk to recall anything. Maybe if you stop with the alcohol for a little, something may dawn upon you," The cop's eye was stuck on the back corner, not blinking just staring.

I peered over my shoulder to see what he was staring at. A few beer cans were scattered in the corner. So what? A few cans here and there didn't mean anything. I stood up in anger.

"How dare you come into my apartment and say I have an alcohol problem- I barely drink, and when I do, I sometimes drink water here and there. I am certainly not an alcoholic. Since you are uninterested in any of this, you can leave my apartment now." Fueled by rage, I stood up and opened the door.

"Don't come back- you'll be interrupting me and my nonalcoholic six pack!"

"Okay ma'am, there is no need to get upset. I think my partner and I have all the information we need. We'll stay in contact."

As the two cops walked out, I let go of the door in hopes it would hit them. *I am not an alcoholic. I can control myself.*

I walked over to my fridge to grab a drink. The popping sound of the twist off cap made my heart skip a beat, or rather my liver. My body perked up, refueling myself from the other night.

With a beer in one hand and Stanley's journal in the other, I began a quick jog to the couch. Throwing myself on the sofa, I started to read. Most of the journals were confusing since they were all worn out. A few words here and there were readable.

Grabbing the last page of the journal by the binding, I flipped through each page to see if any were readable. A few pages of his journal are missing; others, too worn out to even be legible. The few that I could scrap were disoriented. A folded up piece of paper fell out and drifted through the air currents and onto the floor. With a careful touch, I unfolded the paper along the rigid edges that had been torn out of the book. It was in perfect condition like he wrote them yesterday. The black ink vibrantly stood out, illuminating each word so carefully.

January 27ᵗʰ, 1973

I can't sleep. Whenever I close my eyes I think about what happened. Forget sleeping in our- my bed. I can't lie in a bed where Elizabeth and I used to lay. Her perfume was still on the pillows. Strands of her hair still pushed under the pillow. The bedroom was all decorated by Elizabeth. This whole house is Elizabeth. At the time I couldn't have cared less about how the house looked like. I let her detail every corner, every wallpaper, everything. I can't get away- not that I want to. I want her back I can't go on anymore moping around. It's too hard to be surrounded and reminded by her belongings. The other day I was looking at her side of the closet. Her dresses pin straight on the rack. Not a wrinkle that the eye could see. Just like her pillows, the perfume clouded her clothes. My legs quivered and gave out, I fell to the floor. I clung onto her shirts, that flooded the floor of the closet. In the corner was her favorite blue suede skirt she bought for herself after she finished school. She was so happy she saved up for weeks to buy it as a graduation present. Among her shirts, was my shirt I had worn in the accident. I never got to throwing it away. I guess it was the only thing that I have to remember the few moments leading up to what happened. My stomach turned, I began to feel disgusted. Not at her but towards myself. I felt responsible for what happened. I can't look at myself in the mirror. All I see is a monster. I knew it wasn't my fault, but I was the one behind the wheel. I was the one who didn't react and as a result I lost my best friend, the love of my life, the one person who could make me smile and laugh till my stomach hurt. She's gone now and forever.

Then there's Margaret- I can still remember looking in the back seat to see her face. It still haunts me. Knowing I will never be able to see my little girl again. I would never see her graduate, or walk down the aisle. Everything was perfect. Then some idiot had to come along and take it all away from me. I have nothing left.

He goes from talking about his wife and how happy they were to when he was a father and a husband. He had the life that people dream about. The folded up piece of paper had nothing else to it no explanation, nothing. My mind wandered into the possibility of another journal. I needed to know what happened. There has to be more than this crummy piece of paper back in his apartment.

Gently throwing my book onto my bed, I rushed to the door. Getting up too fast made my head pound to the point where opening my eyes felt more like an unwanted chore. I stumbled to my bathroom and chased two Advil with whatever was left in the bottle under the sink. The drink was pungent but nothing I couldn't handle. I longed to hear Stanley yell at me as I went towards his door. My hand on the knob again feeling the same emotions as I did before. Following the books around the baseboard, I began to look for the spot where I can find the other journal. Picking up every book on the floor and along the baseboard, most of the books had nothing to them but blank pages, one book's page is a scribbled out paragraph. For twenty minutes I looked around, to find anything; another journal, a crumpled up piece of paper, even a sign telling me what happened that night. Trying not to tear up his apartment, I began to look with a sense of carefulness. Knowing very little about Stanley I got the feeling that he wouldn't like his things to be out of order. One last stitch effort I went into his bedroom; the central mess of the whole apartment. I look around at the clothes on the ground, the open drawers, and the closet all torn out. My eyes catch on a few books on the inside of his closet. Lined up against the baseboard, just like they were in the living room. Crouching down I picked up all three. Two of them were old, and the last wasn't worn out at all. It had the freshest ink out of all of them. I ran out of his apartment and dropped my books onto the counter. I knew that it would be a long night and I would need a drink or two.

In need of something to soothe the long night, I headed of the convenience store across the street. The automatic doors opened and the fluorescent lights beamed down, almost lighting up my path. I pulled the frosty six pack out of the freezer and headed to the register. As I placed it on the counter, I tried to talk to the clerk.

"So how's your shift tonight going?"

Jack always worked the night shift. Since I came in here more than most, we knew each other quite well.

"Yeah, my night's fine, your total is $9.90," he said, not even paying attention to me.

"Okay, here's a ten. My night's going okay. You know we should hang out sometime. I feel like we have a connection," I mumbled as I took out a crumpled ten dollar bill from my pocket.

"Here's your change, have a good night," He brushed off the question and went back to playing on his phone.

After getting home from the convenience store, I put the pack of beers on the floor and plopped myself onto the sofa; only opening the journal that looks the most worn.

A few journals were legible. Most described his life pre-marriage. How he was always looking for the one. One journal was when Stanley first meeting Elizabeth. He described her as the one right when their eyes locked on one another.

"Last night was the only night that mattered in my life. When I get older and senile, I will always remember tonight. Her name is Elizabeth. I was sitting down at the bar. I had just ordered a Gin Rickey, due to the persistent bartender making me order one, I look over to see this woman standing alone in the corner. Black glasses and a green dress on. It didn't take long before I mustered up the courage to go and talk to her. We sat down at in a booth and talked for three hours straight. Elizabeth is the one."

I never thought about Stanley, but when I did I never had anything nice to say. I guess I never placed him in any other setting. I always thought he was just another grumpy old man waiting around doing nothing, passing time till he dies. It struck me that this man had a life, a good too. I threw the old warped journal to the floor and picked up the second one. This one had three entries in it. All from different years, 1952,1953,1954. The first entry was all about his first year dating Elizabeth. They cherished every moment and all that fantasy bs. Stanley and Elizabeth got married in 1953, the following year his wife was pregnant with Margaret. The two seemed so in love. They were happy with each other.

I was halfway done with my 4th beer when I grabbed the last journal. My hands started to shake and my vision began to be blurry. I overcame the obstacles to read one last journal before I pass out. It was labeled

April 9th, 2016, only a few months ago. Reading it to myself, wasn't working. I kept reading the same line over and over again to understand. Reading out loud made a little more sense.

"April 9th, 2016

I have gone a very long time not writing in these journals. The compel of writing withered away after a while. My daily activities didn't interest me enough to write about them. Every day is the same now. Repetition will lead me to death. I have become numb to the outside world, the technology and way of life does not interest me. The only thing that does bother me is my neighbor, Emily. She's a very high strung and odd woman. Almost every night she comes home around two A.M. stumbles to try and find her keys. She usually passes out outside of her door. I always go out and unlock her door while she's sleeping so that she doesn't have a problem in the morning. Maybe it's because I have no one or maybe it's because she reminds me of Margaret. Always wanting to go her way, and being stubborn on every topic. I just don't understand how on abuses alcohol like that. I was never a fan of the taste but when I did I cherished it. A few sips here and there to appreciate the body and the texture of every different drink. I can still remember the taste of the champagne I had at my wedding and the first time I ever had a beer. How can one even tolerate that much in their liver-"

He doesn't even know me and he thinks I have a problem, that's it Stanley whoever the hell you even are this drink goes to you!

I get up to crack open the last two beers, drinking to the last drop of each. The bottles drop to the floor, glass everywhere. I throw the journal to the corner landing right in the middle of the binding. My eyes grow heavy and the room begins to go dark. I fall back into the couch passing as the last beer falls out of my hand.

The next morning I woke up with my head pounding yet again. I stumbled as I got up trying to avoid the broken glass on the floor. I passed the mirror in the way to the kitchen, looking down to not see what I looked like. I drank a bottle of water to hydrate then tried to clean up the mess from last night. I swept up the glass and threw away the other bottles. I picked up the journal in the corner. It flipped to the page I left off on. Only reading Stanley bashing me, I disregarded the part where he actually cared about me.

"I wish she would just realize that she does have a problem. I would say something if she didn't always attack me with her vicious tongue. Everyday it's something new and vulgar. I do care for her in a neighborly way-"

Each journal had chipped away a block of negativity that I had thought about him. He actually cared about me in some way. I had never felt like this before. I wanted to stop drinking but never really had a reason. Stanley is that something in my life I had longed for. I decided that the only way I could fix things was to see Stanley face to face.

I rushed to the hospital in hopes to find him. After reading bits and pieces of his life story I knew I had to actually meet this man. The lady at the front desk buried her head in her phone and disregarding anything that came her way.

"Hello, is there a Stanley Whitmore here? He was brought here this morning. I need to see him immediately." The sweat on my palms started to drip of the counter as I gripped onto the counter.

"Good afternoon ma'am, how can I help you?" She kept a straight face, not even a blink came out of her, as if she doesn't work in a place where people are sick

"First it's miss not ma'am but that's a different conversation. Yeah, I'm looking for a Stanley Whitmore. He was rushed here this morning; can you tell me where I can find him?"

"Oh I'm sorry but I can't reveal patient information unless you are related to him?"

"Um, yes I am. I am his daughter," I couldn't think of anything else to say in a moment's time so I had to lie. Not thinking of the end result and the problems I could run into later.

"Well in that case, I can direct you to the third floor where all the new patients are taken. There you can ask the head nurse if the person you are looking for is there."

"Okay, thank you," I ran towards the elevator with my head still aching with a tolerable throbbing. My heart beats in anticipation, but also trembles for the unknown fear. What if he doesn't want to see me? What if he doesn't understand why I'm here? What if he gets mad that I read his journals? What if he isn't--

"Hi, can I help you?" A student volunteer asked as I turned the corner

"No, well yeah I guess. I'm looking for a Stanley Whitmore. He should be around this floor,"

My eye wondering looking in each room to see if he's was in one of them

"I don't think there is a Stanley Whitmore on this floor anymore, but I could check for you."

Anymore? What did that mean? The student volunteer walked over the one of the nurses at the desk. A slight murmur and exchange of glances turned my fate.

The volunteer came back with that look on her face that means they are uncomfortable but hey have no

"So it looks like Stanley is not on the floor anymore. Stanley passed last night. Since you aren't on the visiting list I can't tell you anymore information."

I walked away not listening to the rest of her common sad spiel. I had come all this way to see him and he's dead. I couldn't believe it. I got sober for nothing and yet again someone leaves me. I am done with it all. Taking the elevator down each tick signifying the floors grew silent as I thought about what could've happened. My hopes were too high, it wasn't like we were going to hold hands and reminisce about the past. As I walk out of the elevator to the garage, my eye catches the mini mart.

To hell with it.

The automatic doors open and I head to the back of the store. The neon lights direct my path. With each step I take, I can taste it in my mouth. I reach out to the freezer. I take out a single can and slowly open it. I appreciate it, the popping sound all the way to the fizzing dying out. I held the can up to my lips and left out a breath of air said-

Cheers.

Give Me Liberty

I don't think I'll ever really get used to it here. It's not the same as being up in my home, boy do I miss that place. Now I guess I've just become a part of the history- it's a shame, but at this point, my usefulness has expired. If only I could go back-back to when I was used, back before this awful scar, back before everyone had these bright little devices they can't keep their noses out of, that was when I mattered. It seemed just yesterday that people would hear my calls and come in from miles around. That was always a sight to see. Watching hundreds, even thousands, of people fill in all around the stage to listen to just one man. I haven't seen that in years.

It was much more refreshing than these shined granite walls and this dastardly steel confinement. I'd give anything to be back in the Steeple. Seeing the miles of land and all the people would always remind me of why I was there. It reminded me of my purpose-the purpose that was so wrongfully stripped from me.

Either way, so many people pass through here in a day, it doesn't matter any more. I've seen every kind of person there is to see at this point. Most of the time, it's kids walking by, ill-concerned with what the inscriptions mean and more focused on getting out of school for a day. All they ever do is take a picture and leave. They know nothing of what I was-such a shame- if only they knew!

On the other hand, there are people who wanted to know or knew about me and what I represented. The tour guides and teachers were the ones who actually understood. Often, kids would come up and think they knew it all. Any answer to any of the same questions, as if they could tell the difference between Washington and Jackson.

Even if I didn't know them personally, they were as sure as my copper important as I was I've learned a lot from people over the years, as dull as they've become.

I watched as a group of students approached, led by an older, curly-haired woman. It seemed this was the first class trip of today.

"Can anybody tell me when this was originally hung?" I heard the woman say. They all stared blankly at her.

"C'mon, no one even has a guess? Remember, it's older than anyone standing here right now." Did they really not know? Not even the time period! Surprisingly, one of them, in the center of the group, was brave enough to raise his hand instead of looking down at his black box.

"1983?" he said timidly.

The schooling system has definitely gone downhill, that's for sure. Everyone used to be so well spoken and knowledgeable. Now because of their Goggle and Tweeter, it's like they don't care anymore. You had to make the effort for the information back then. Now in this...age of information, no one has to go to their library and retrieve what they were looking for. Everything seems to be right in their shining box.

She laughed, "Umm... no. Close, but you're off by about 200 years, anyone else?" she continued, looking around for a slightly more intelligent answer.

1753. It cannot be that hard to remember four numbers. I thought everyone would know this. It's even on the papers they're given-not that they care much for them. By the time they leave, I'm sure almost all of them will find their way to the ground.

"No one?" she questioned, looking defeated.

"Well, even though we went over this on the bus here, I'll jog your memory. 1753 was the year it was hung in Independence Hall."

That was ages ago. Nothing went to plan on that day. They tried to be careful as they hooked me up, high above the city. It felt good to be up there, almost as if it was what I was made for- I was meant to be hung up there. That day the waiting was the worst. All the measuring and making sure everything was just right. The only thing that rivaled it was having to hear all these agonizing questions each day.

Once they'd finished all the measurements, it finally happened- I was hung up for everyone to see. I'd still be there if it weren't for this damned scar.

It was up there that my first laceration was oh so lovingly bestowed upon me. Those fools wanted to test my sound. They pulled the rope and watched as I swung in place, humming my beautiful note. It was a good feeling, to finally be in use. I rang as loud as my metal would allow for all to hear.

A few rings in, and my voice became sharply off key, as the sound was replaced with an unforgettable sharp pain that coursed through me. It was unbearable, as if lightning was shooting up my body. I could do nothing but stare at the horror on the men's faces as they realized what they've done. They stopped my swaying and pondered what to do with me. I couldn't believe they had let this happen. After all the preparation, all the transporting and checking, I was ready to be what this country needed me to be, and they took it from me. Those damned fools wouldn't have known a cowbell from a sleigh bell, let alone how to care for me.

As expected, they ran to go get help. It was torment seeing more and more people in high-priced suits and wigs come up and give me an offended look. As if my mere existence was now a burden. There was chatter and mumbles coupled with an overwhelming sense of panic filling the steeple.

They eventually came to the conclusion to leave me hanging where I was until they could figure out what to do next. I'm not entirely sure what became of the men who turned me from symbol to trouble.

"Oh wow, so this is almost as old as you, huh, Mrs. Jackson?" piped one of the children.

How rude to say, especially to an upstanding woman such as herself. The rest of them erupted with laughter. Who do they think they are? She's a respected woman; leave her be.

"Now, now, I'm not quite as old as our bell here, but does anyone know who was?" There are thousands of people my age, yet none of them are around anymore. The only ones I knew, personally, however, were those who rang me, but even then, I didn't really know them. The only one I remember is the one who moved me here. He's the one who embedded this feeling into my tin. This emptiness I can't get rid of.

"Is it your husband?" chimed one of the girls.

There was another round of laughter. Had they said that in my time, they would've been corrected immediately and never said anything like that again.

"Pass and Stau! Stoo? I forget," said the child in the middle.

"Yes, Tommy!" she happily cheered.

"Mr. Pass and Mr. Stow! their names are engraved right into the front of the bell, see?" She gestured toward me. They all looked and squinted to read my faded out writing.

❧ ❧

I remember meeting the acquaintance of John Pass and John Stow. These two "ingenious work-men," as Isaac Norris called them in his letter, did a fine job of fixing the mess the others had created. When I was brought to them, it was easy to see how nervous they were. They knew they had a big task to handle and the weight of it showed on their faces. If they made any error, it would most likely mean the end of their work in this business- after all, who would hire someone who ruined the country's staple of liberty?

However, after the hours of arguing and work, I looked perfectly new again. They undoubtedly lived up to their titles, being able to solve all my problems with a single remedy. They masterfully crafted a mixture of liquid and copper in order to make me stronger. It reinforced my structure and made me uncrack able. There was no more gash and my color was just as perfect as before. I almost had half the mind to forgive the ones who cracked me in the first place But just as quickly as they smoothed out my crack, they thought it was a good idea to carve their names into my body-being so proud of themselves for their work, they felt it necessary to brand me and now I'll forever be associated with those two names.

Yet, once I was back where I was meant to be, my sound wasn't the same. My voice sounded far less like liberty ringing through the city and more like a bell meant for mourning. Yet again, I went back to Mr. Pass and Mr. Stow so they could, yet again, fix me. Hopefully, correctly, this time. Except, instead of adding to me or changing what they used, they chipped away at me. Literally, piece by piece, they took me apart, and reassembled me, changing me. And this was all for the sake of the tone. I fought through the pain, simply to be what I was destined to be.

After I was recast a second time, they hung me up again, right where I should be. I remained a symbol, giving hope to the people that needed it and would serve my purpose. Despite my flawed sound, every time someone rang me from that point on, more and more people would come to watch. I was the city's celebrity; newspapers coined me "the highest note of liberty." I meant something to people then - if only that same sentiment rang true today

"Now, does anybody know what this was actually used for?" she asked.

Again, she was going with very broad questions. There practically wasn't anything I didn't ring for, but my curiosity to their answers held my attention. One of them raised their hand, still looking down at their glowing box.

"Yes, Molly? What do you think?" she said expectantly.

"It is an iconic symbol of American in-dee-pen-dance, located in Phil-lee-dal-phi-a, Pennsylvania. Formerly placed in the steeple of the Pennsylvania State Ho-"

"Thank you, I can read Wikipedia, too. Not what I'm looking for though," The woman interrupted, and rightfully so. She could've easily said "to ring," and she would've gotten credit. Instead, she's using her glowing-hand-device as a crutch. How shocking.

"You do know this; it's actually right in front of you. Did you guys not read the handout?"

She waved a paper around in the air. How couldn't they know? I'm one of the oldest pieces of American history, not only should I be taught, but memorized. This ignorance hurts worse than the scar did when it first happened. These arrogant kids always think they know best. Anything older than them is outdated and practically useless. If only they saw me in my prime, they'd have more of an appreciation for who I am.

"It was meant to bring people together, right?" said Thomas, looking at me hopefully.

"Right again, Tommy!" she said with glee. This one seemed to be different than the rest. He's the average size, but had a certain gleam in his stare that the others didn't seem to possess. "The Liberty Bell was used to summon lawmakers and government officials to discuss what was going on in the government!" she reiterated. "You guys who don't know this might find it wise to write this down."

Immediately, their wooden quills were on paper. Yet again, the woman was right.

The first time I ever assembled the public was quite some time after I was hung. It was for a soldier, reading something. A declaration of the sorts. He was very passionate about it, whatever it was. Everyone seemed so joyous that day that their cheers were unforgettable. I can still hear them shouting about "taxes" and "freedom". I felt fulfilled then, as if my purpose was complete. The following years were very much filled with that same enthusiasm. Everyone seemed happier and genuinely excited to be where they were, shouting about being apart of the "best damned country this world has to offer." It was refreshing to see all those fine people as happy as they were.

That shift in the energy is something I could only imagine spread throughout the whole country. There were systems being put in place and work being done. This momentum lasted for several decades. Every time they needed me to ring, I rang loud and true throughout the entire city, no one could mistake my sound. I rang through wars, through turmoil, rain, sleet, snow- anything. I rang. I took comfort in knowing that these people cared enough about their country to want to make a change, and I would bring them together to do just that.

"Next question, who knows how, and when, it got its crack?" said the woman.

The children, yet again, were obviously struggling. I wouldn't. I know exactly where this came from. This horrid scar that put me here. I remember each and every detail of that day.

"Is it because someone broke it?" said the one from the middle again. That was certainly one way to put it, dear Thomas.

"Well...yes, however tell me a little more," she said.

What else could you want to know? That my pre-existing cracks weren't taken care of properly? That the bellman pulled the rope too hard?

"Is it because someone threw it on the ground?" chimed another.

That was just false. To imagine, someone dropping me. They would've been killed back then.

"One more guess! Who else wants to take a stab at it?" she sang.

They all looked at each other, dumbfounded. As if there was no other option than what they've said.

"We talked about them earlier!" They all stood still, almost paralyzed by their own ignorance. "Well, it got it's crack on a very important day. It was the birthday of our first president! George.." she trailed off.

"Bush!" shouted one of the taller ones.

"No, not George Bush, sweetie." she corrected him. To watch the way everything changes in a mere instant simply by the head of our proud country changing is astounding. The way these people talk and act towards each other, it all changes with the election. It's a miracle these kids even knew we had presidents before that Clinton boy.

"It was George Washington!" she chimed, acting as if this crowd knew who he was. From what I've learned, he was one of the most revolutionary people in history and they don't even know who he was. Pitiful. "It was on his birthday that the Bell cracked."

I may not have met the man, but I know everything I can about him. Hearing these tours pass through, I know everything from his height to how many years he served the country.

To no surprise, she was right. They wanted to commemorate his being alive. I heard him give speeches, watched him shake hands, he was a good man. Yet I still can't deny that I had hatred built towards him. It was his fault I was ringing with a cracked crown that day. It was his fault that I sit here as a relic instead of the symbol I was. It was of no matter now, those years have been long passed. Now I'm meant to enrich the education of these children.

◈ ◈

"Finally, does anyone have any questions?" asked the woman.

I could only imagine what's racing through their heads. There was so much unanswered or that had gone unmentioned. She didn't even begin to mention how I came to be here. She forgot about how I was in the State House and why they never fixed me again. Why they cursed me to sit here forever, watching the unawareness peruse in and out of my center.

But as I've seen these children walk by, there's almost never one who wants to learn of me. Not too often would a childlike Thomas come along. Someone interested in what I mean. It's easy to tell what kind of person they'll be as soon as they walk in. The look in their eye determines their thoughts for the next 15 minutes. The way they look at me, as if I was still in the Steeple. That's the reason I'm still here.

"Alright guys, let's get going." said the woman. "We don't have all day and this bell isn't going anywhere. So, let's go see Independence Hall!"

They all filed away, one by one through the door while she kept rattling off facts about our history. I watched their eyes go down and look into their black boxes one more time. Once again, I was left alone.

"Hey," said a small voice.

It was Thomas. He was looking at me with a hope and admiration I haven't seen in years. It was almost touching.

"I know they don't care about you, but I do," he whispered, taking a step forward.

He looked around at the rest of the center like he was searching for someone. The only other person here was the policeman standing outside the front.

After assuring he was alone, he smiled. Very quickly, he ducked under the metal guard rails and approached me.

What is he going to do? I thought. No one had gotten this close in years; I could practically feel his breath running down my crown.

He brought his hand up in a fist, with purpose burning in his eyes and, with a flick of his wrist, I rang again.

Broken Records

My body was rejecting all the cheap liquor I had drowned it with in the most brutal way. The trash can next to my bed filled with the remnants of last night's binge, while I was still dressed in yesterday's clothes. I wiped the black makeup that was smeared around my eyes, hoping for my hazy vision to clear. Laying there, consumed by agony, my half-conscious self realized that today was the tomorrow that I was dreading.

"You look like hell, Naomi," Anna deliberately expressed. Her blonde hair was tied back by a rainbow colored scrunchie and her makeup-less face looked unsettlingly pale and exhausted. A *Madonna Virgin Tour* shirt hung off her shoulders while she hustled towards the kitchen sink. As she turned around, my eyes immediately focused in on the glass of water she was carrying in her hand. I felt my tongue brush against the roof of my mouth like two pieces of sandpaper rubbing against one another. Eager to chug that heavenly glass of water, I let out a distasteful groan and draped my head along the side of the bed where the early morning sun shone through like a blinding laser beam.

"I look it, and I feel like I'm in it, Anna," I said while using all of my strength to lift my arm and grasp the glass of water she waved in front of me. As I pushed my untamed hair away from my face, I sat up slowly and watched the tangled sheets fall to the floor. As the water cleansed the acid in my throat and stomach, Anna stood tall before me, as if she had prepared a staged intervention.

"On my way home from class last night, I found you passed out with an empty bottle of booze cuddled against your chest," Anna said while staring at the floor. My gut wrenched as I anticipated what was to come of this already shameful and embarrassing conversation. Although Anna had a kind nature, I could sense that she was on the verge of putting her foot down like an angry parent would to their troublesome child.

"Anna, I am so sor—" Before I could fully apologize, I was cut off by her intrusive voice.

"I understand that you are experiencing a rough time with dropping out and all, but this is the fourth time this has happened this week—" I cut Anna off, preventing my ears from hearing the humiliating fact that was about to pour out of her mouth.

"I'm going to get it together real soon I-I promise," I was tongue-tied, but managed to squeeze those words out.

"The fourth," Anna declared as I felt my tired eyes droop. I was unsure if she had repeated those last two words, or if my clouded mind had played that phrase over again to enhance the throbbing headache I was already experiencing.

I felt a burst of vomit engulf my throat as my poisoned stomach clenched. Daunting images of myself alone and unconscious in the dark alleyways of Boston or with my frail body passed out in some dive bar began to flood my dazed mind.

"Naomi, what are you planning to do with your life now?" Anna blurted out with a subtle frustration taking over her usual relaxed tone of voice. I felt the consequence of my choices pounding even more violently in my head.

She plopped herself on the stool diagonal from my bed and continued on with her spiel, as if she hadn't realized that I was already emotionally and physically beaten to a pulp.

"I understand that this talk is certainly not the icing on the top of the cake for you, but I haven't received your rent money for two whole months now— and while I am your roommate, I did not sign up to be your babysitter," Anna expressed as her forehead tightened with worry lines. I slammed the heavy glass against the large vinyl which sat on my night stand, causing it to crack in half. In all my misery, I began to make my way to the bathroom as a feeling of shame pulsed through me.

"Naomi, I need the money by the end of the week. If that's not possible, then I think it's time for you to consider finding a new place," Anna hastily declared. With my feet planted on the ground and back facing her, I twisted my neck and turned my head in an attempt to make eye contact. She sat on her stool, like a queen sitting on her throne, and I, the poor peasant she was so cruelly turning away.

As I walked past the television, I focused my attention in on the music video playing on MTV to avoid what Anna had proposed. Continuing my way to the bathroom, I stumbled over my now useless college textbooks and felt my body which was painted in shades of blues and blacks crash against the floor. How I got those bruises is a mystery, one that I am entirely unwilling to investigate further. Despite being stripped of all my dignity, I stood back up and headed towards the shower to clean up the one and last mess I had control over in my life. I left Anna in a deafening silence and saved my whimpering tears for the shower.

After a frigid cold shower to help awaken my mind and recover my body from the hurricane of last night's alcohol endeavor, I was cruelly accompanied by Anna's new CD player playing some hip-hop. Frustration welted up inside of me as I clenched my fist in an effort to bite my tongue and refrain from ruining our now rocky relationship. She knew how much I despised CD's, and how their invention was leaving me unemployed, seemingly robbing me of my job, and now, my life.

In a hurry to get to work, I tore my closet open and threw on the first shirt I saw while mistakenly spotting one of my favorite Boston College tees. That sight tugged at my heart, reminding me that all I aspired to be in life had crumbled to dust. Coincidentally, when records stopped spinning, my zest for life came to a halt, as well—I lost my passion for learning, and all the inspiration that my prior self once contained.

The streets were desolate and cold that morning. As I turned the corner, I noticed that the store's sign appeared different than the way it used to. *Best of Bean Town's Used Records* did not ring with the same fluidity that it previously had. Beneath the shop's name a sign which wrote in bulging red letters, "Going out of business, everything 50% off or more" hung in the glass window. The two statements clashed; from the best of Beantown, to the obvious worst case scenario for a business.

It was disheartening to know that timeless records held no value compared to the new and dull way of listening to music through CD's and cassette tapes.

"Hey girl, is it cool if I leave you to clean and mark up the rest of the records alone today?" My boss approached me as I entered through the bell sounding door. Daisy was the most lively elder woman I had ever known. It was evident that she had a young soul from her decision to wear bedazzled jeans and by the way she chose to get rid of her grey hair by dying it bright pink.

"I got it covered Daisy, don't worry, I can close up tonight too," I responded. It felt surprisingly refreshing to have an entire afternoon to throw on some old records, get a little tipsy, and purposefully work in the calm company of my own solitary.

"I trust you with my records, and honey that's a whole lot of trust 'cause they're my babies. Mark em' up for sale at whatever price you think— but hun, please don't give away any freebies," She chuckled, echoing the rough and uneasy sound of a smoker's laugh.

"Oh, and it'll be your last shift babe. The era of Boston's greatest used vinyl shop ends tomorrow. You and I are taking home whatever doesn't sell," Daisy exclaimed. A somber and vacant feeling suddenly filled the once vibrant and booming store. We then exchanged a look of sadness, both of us unwilling to let go of all the memories tied to our workplace.

"Screw you CD's for taking my business!" Daisy shouted as she waved both her middle fingers in the air. Although she intended for this to be a harmless expression of humor, I saw the pure defeat in her eyes.

Once I heard the shop door click I hurried to the back room to quench my unrelenting thirst for some booze. I glanced at *The Beatles* record which hung on the wall and felt my tear ducts trigger. The day I met Daisy was the day I fell in love with that band and relied on music as my security.

The record store was a sensation—the craze of every college student in the city. My first visit was spent standing there doe-eyed, uptight and unsure of what to check out while others filled the store with their echoing laughs and good riddance.

"Don't carry the world upon your shoulders" a woman with streaked blonde and baby blue hair softly sang as she walked past my young, re-served self.

"You look like you could use it, babe," a once carefree Daisy ex-claimed as she forced a Beatles record in my one of my hands, while I tugged on my hair out of nervousness with the other.

Soon enough, the time that I had spent studying textbooks was replaced with playing records.

I pressed my palm against my cheek, pondering how everything turned upside down within a mere three years.

CD's are the silent killer—they are the ones to blame. I thought as I studied the record on the wall which brought me to Daisy years back.

I kept my bottle close by and arranged a sneaky hiding spot in case a customer were to stop in. As I watched city slickers motion by the window with CD's and cassettes in hand, I gulped down some liquor and felt it sting my tongue and aggravate my throat.

The store was dead, and so were records.

While chronologically categorizing the records I grew more de-pressed. It was as if an icicle had grown inside of me, poking at my heart and causing my soul to become bitterly cold. The blurrier my vision became, the more aware I grew of how truly lost I was. As the sunset illuminated the store, I took in the sight knowing that it would be the last glimpse of light that I'll ever see shine through that big storefront window.

I came across a heaping amount of Elvis records, took a few more swigs, and then focused in on the tedious task at hand. The vinyls had a soothing texture, a familiar and satisfying feeling that I wasn't ready to let go of. After dusting off Elvis' *Crying in the Chapel* record, I glanced down at my overalls and noticed a black and white photograph which had fallen right onto my lap. I held up the photograph in one hand while tightly grasping my bottle with the other.

Brown rust coated the top left corner of the photograph and the edges were worn to the extent where it felt as if the picture was about to crumble in my hand. The image of the young and carefree woman should have ignited my soul with a feeling of happiness. Rather, I was consumed by envy over that gleaming smile she had across her face and the two carefree peace signs she held up.

I pressed my legs up against my chest and rested my back against the shelf. Although I was surrounded by piles of records, I felt as if I were in an empty space, entirely deserted from the world. I took another sip and felt a single tear stream down my cheek and watched as it wet the paper bag that covered my bottle. I went to place the photograph down and noticed scratchy handwriting on the back.

I zoomed in my eyes to the words like a focused camera lens, ready to capture a moment. Attentively and carefully, my drunken voice mumbled out loud,

To my Daisy,

Like a river flows surely to the sea, darling so it goes, some things are meant to be.

You will find your way, my love.
J.C

I stared blankly at the stack of records as my brain made an immediate connection. Suddenly, I felt revived by this photograph which had coincidentally landed in my lap. The same woman who had thrown her middle fingers up to the sky this morning had once held up peace signs while beaming ear to ear. I held those words and her smiling face in my hand as I gently pressed my head against the cold black and white tile floors, with a stack of records blanketing me for the night.

When I woke the next morning, I wasn't accompanied by the usual aches and pains which typically followed a night of drowning in my sorrows. I stood up in awe of my will to continue forward and picked up the bottle which contained a mere few sips left. I glanced at the photograph of an ecstatic Daisy and carefully held it against my chest.

I placed the photograph of a young Daisy back where I had found it and left my key to the store on top of the stack of Elvis records. As I opened the door, the bell rang the with the same familiar sound it always had, yet, it sounded entirely unfamiliar. I held the bottle of liquor down by my side while taking in one last glimpse of the place that I had once known to be so alive—the place that was once filled with used and loved records. I then left the record store behind and felt a gust of wind hit my back from the heavy door which shut and locked behind me. Without a particular direction in mind to walk on that street, I decided that I should first kick my unfinished bottle to the curb.

A Blackened Memory

I *have to get to my 8 am.* That thought awakened Alec from a deep sleep, and struck him with an immediate panicky sweat. As he yawned, forcing a massive gust of air into his lungs, his tired eyes opened and glimpsed at the early morning sun's reflection on the oak floor. Confused as to why his alarm hadn't gone off, Alec glanced at the bulging red numbers on the clock, which read 7:48.

"Dammit," he mumbled as he violently tossed the comforter aside and thrust his body out of a sea of white silk sheets.

"Honey, your meeting was cancelled," Laila's soft voice echoed throughout the walls of their flat apartment. "Oh and Pat called, he said there's no need to go into the office today."

Alec's thumping heart slowed as his angsty breathing began to calm. Before launching himself back into bed, a doubtful thought instantly flooded his mind. A suspicious Alec decided to give Pat a call himself. The chances of his important business meeting being cancelled was odd. Even an exuberant Alec was unable to relinquish in the news until his concern was put to rest.

Alec was stopped right in his tracks by Laila who swatted his hand as he reached for the telephone which was mounted on the wall. He was taken aback by both her forceful reaction, and the noticeable dark bags which hung beneath her eyes like two heavy, dark clouds in the sky right before a storm. They made her appear exhausted and worn out, which was a rare appearance for his typically energetic and lively wife to display. Alec wondered why that sparkle in her eyes seemed to be drastically duller this morning.

"Pat's visiting with family in Connecticut, he said that there is no reason to call back, and to enjoy a well-deserved day off," she pronounced those words as if it were a redundant script she'd practiced a million times over before. Alec raised his eyebrow with suspicion as his annoyed wife grabbed his unshaved face and plopped a kiss on his right cheek. Laila's mood had flipped a switch within a mere split second which caused Alec to fret.

"Huh, okay," Alec said as he wiped his cheek which was damp from her kiss. A day off from his demanding job would usually relieve some of the overwhelming amount of stress which weighed heavily on his shoulders. Alec knew that it was unlike him to question this news twice, but for some unexplainable reason, an instinctive feeling rose within him. Despite what he had been told, Alec felt that he was still needed at the office.

He sat on the edge of his king sized bed, pondering what his day would entail. Walking into the room, he saw Laila with her robe and slippers on, her hands grasping onto a steaming cup of green tea-the same cup she drank from each morning.

"Where's my suit? I could've sworn you ironed and hung it up in the closet last night," he asked, observing Laila's face tighten with worry.

"Ale, I put it away for you this morning, ya know, after Pat called the house. Besides you won't be needing it today. How about I make us a nice breakfast while you just worry about relaxing," Laila exclaimed with an irritated attitude, masked behind a sweet tone of voice.

"Well that sounds nice," Alec responded as Laila turned her back to place her cup of tea on the dresser.

She frantically searched for a coaster between the stacks of books and magazines with one hand, while chaotically spilling droplets of tea onto the floor with the other.

"In sickness and in health, every damn day," she mumbled under her breath as another droplet of green tea splashed against the hardwood floor.

"What'd you say?" Alec quickly interrogated her. Laila turned around, as if she'd been caught red-handed.

"I was just talking to myself. I said, where are those damn coasters?" she quickly responded, flashing a mischievous smile at him.

While Laila showered, Alec dug threw his closet and picked out the sharpest looking unironed suit he could find. His eyes squinted and forehead formed into tiny, stress lines as he gently wiped a dust stain off the shoulder of his black suit jacket. An always polished and put together Alec was troubled by a closet full of wrinkled, dusty attire.

After putting the suit on and buttoning each button one by one, Alec called his driver for a ride, who strangely did not answer. Alec stared at the phone in his hand with pure confusion when there wasn't even a "beep" to leave a message. After he tied his red silk tie, and finished buttoning the sleeves of his suit jacket, he stood in front of his bathroom mirror to gel his hair. While pushing his jet black hair back, his eye caught onto a gashing scar on the middle of his scalp, where his hairline began. His jaw dropped as he pressed his head closer to the mirror, studying and poking at the large white scar like a scientist prods and pokes at an experiment. Alec wondered how he went about life without noticing this massive defect on the middle of his head.

Amidst this perplexed situation, Alec washed his hands which were greasy and covered with hair gel, and figured that the scar had truly never caught his attention. While standing beside the marble table where his briefcase was routinely placed, Alec began to jot down a quick note to Laila which read, *Went to work. Be home later, my love.* He grabbed the handle of his briefcase which had felt significantly lighter than usual and put the note in place of it.

While Alec whistled for a cab, he noticed the skyscrapers reflection off of one another above like mirrors. *Just another New York day* he thought as he shoved his tie into his buttoned suit to prevent it from being whisked around in the wind. Alec stood pridefully, and watched as the taxi pulled up against the sidewalk.

"I'm going to the Twin Towers sir—Fulton Street," Alec stated as he motioned his body into the cramped back seat of the cab and carefully placed his briefcase on his lap. Alec lifted his briefcase and squinted his eyes with concern, wondering why it had felt so light. Cracking it open, he found nothing inside. Not a single piece of paper or even a pen. That rush of panic that he experienced earlier in the morning came back. His head shook back and forth as anxious thoughts began to ruminate in his mind. Alec laid the briefcase opened on the seat of the taxi beside him, and nervously twiddled his thumbs as he focused his thoughts on his papers' whereabouts.

"'Em here you are sir, the memorial," the driver said while signaling with his hand. Alec peered out the window expecting to see New Yorkers flooding in and out of the south tower entrance. He blinked twice to assure himself that what lay outside of the taxi window was not a figment of his imagination.

"No sir, I didn't ask— ugh. Please take me to The World Trade Center on 285 Fulton Street," a frustrated Alec demanded. He brushed the driver's mistake aside and figured that he had little-to-no experience with the English language.

"I keep meter running or eh, you go," The driver exclaimed as he stared into Alec's dark eyes with a cold expression through the rearview mirror. Alec furiously grabbed his briefcase and threw a wad of crumpled up cash at the hostile taxi driver.

As the cab sped away, Alec's brain went into a frenzy. His empty briefcase slipped through his fingers as he stood there frozen, like a statue. The briefcase crashed and broke open on the hard cement as his eyes stared at the gaping hole ahead. The same briefcase that had once been filled to the brim with work was now laid out on the New York pavement open, dark, and empty, for the world to see. He pressed his right hand on the left side of his chest, feeling his heartbeat grow rapid. Alec's knees trembled as he motioned towards the large square waterfall in the center of lower Manhattan.

Where am I? What is happening? Alec thought as his bloodshot eyes stared at the majestic water trickling down into the square. He stumbled closer, inching his way towards this unfamiliar scene that was on a street which was a second home to Alec. He pressed his hand against the gray plaques and felt the dark, cold stone spark at the end of his fingertips. As he read over the names he gracefully dragged his hand across and felt a bittering, cold confusion.

Patrick Wilkerson

Alec read. He paused with his fingers sprawled out alongside his business partner's name. His mouth plopped open and his eyes began to mock the waterfall which lay directly in before him.

Alec slammed his fist against that cold, dark plaque. Feeling his frustration smash into bits and pieces of pure black ash.

"Alec!" Laila sped through the crowd of people with a pink scarf tied around her wet brown hair. Alec turned around with a face full of tears and the expression of an abandoned and fearful child on his face. Laila threw herself at Alec and latched onto his forearms arms, while attempting to catch her breath.

"I can't think. What is all of this, what is happening?" He sobbed. Alec's voice became faint, it seemed that he was about to drop to the ground in an instant. She grabbed his hands and looked directly into his sobbing brown eyes.

"Listen to me, and breathe," Laila persisted as she tugged on his hand.

"There was a terrorist attack on The Twin Towers on September 11, 2001," Laila said as she watched Alec's red face immediately turn pale white.

"At 8:45 in the morning, when the planes hit, you took a blow in the head. Honey—the injury caused your condition, anterograde amnesia," she tiredly expressed. Alec stood there stunned and dumbfounded, his world suddenly came crashing down and his mind was firing with questions and frustrations.

"Each morning when you wake up, all you are able to recall are the events right before the injury," Laila's voice quivered, but she was clearly fighting to remain calm and stoic. It was evident that she rarely had to explain this to him, but on the days that she did, it was a task that consumed every ounce of her soul.

"It's been over a decade, Alec," she quietly said while staring down at the cement.

A devastated Alec shared a taxi with his wife, only breaking the harsh silence with hard hitting questions, which she was clearly uninterested in answering. He left his open and empty briefcase at Ground Zero, where his memory and life stood damaged and impacted forever.

❦   ❦

Alec laid awake in his bed that night, resenting his lack of control over knowledge or memory. Each night as he dozed off to sleep, his memory crumbled to ash and went completely black. He closed his eyes, aware of the fate that lay before him the next morning—

I have to get to my 8 am. Alec was awakened by this thought.

Lessons

I had that hunk of metal trailered home, having the tow truck driver drop it right in our gated driveway.

"Looks like you guys are pretty well off living here, what are you doing driving this piece of garbage?" the forthright tow truck driver said to me. I shrugged and told him my plan to give it to my son. My wife, Denise, stepped outside and laid her eyes on my first car.

"Well, he's certainly going to be shocked", she said, referring to our brat of a son.

Stepping inside, thoughts raced through my head about what this might teach Steve. Maybe this would be the thing that finally taught him that he'd need to work for what he wanted. It was time for him to learn about independence and responsibility.

"Steven!" I called up our winding spiral stairs- no response, so I called again, met with the same resounding silence. Breathing in to yell up again, my phone illuminated interrupting me with a quick vibration, followed by a beeping noise. "Yes?" read a text message from my son.

"Are you kidding me?" I asked my wife, turning the phone so that she could see the laziness that had become our son. I wasn't looking for an answer, but how could he be so lethargic to not even come down the stairs.

"How did he get this lazy?' she asked.

"I'm not sure but it's time for things to change".

I simply texted back, "I bought you a new car". Before I even realized the message had sent, I heard him running down the stairs. The

217

hard pounding that reverberated off the walls of the staircase foretold the excitement that was about to take place. It reminded me of when he was younger, how he'd dart downstairs on Christmas Day to see all the presents wrapped under the tree. He was always so happy and grateful for his gifts. But it seemed that as his voice changed, becoming deeper, his excitement left as his gratitude became more shallow.

Should I have bought him a new car? I thought to myself. *Would he treat us better?*

As Steven was growing up, it was apparent that his mother and I were to blame as much as he was for the way he'd turned out. The best memories I had with him didn't come from baseball games or in Boy Scouts. Instead, they were from the few times that he'd visit me at the office, either for a quick dinner before a meeting or the few times he'd come to visit me at work with coffee. For all the success I'd created and the wealth our family had come to know, it hadn't transpired into a better connection with our son.

When I turned 16, I saved every penny I could to buy my first car. She didn't run, but when I trailered her home, that Rusty 1970 Plymouth 'Cuda was my pride and joy. My mother was so proud of my hard work, that she ended up wanting to store the car in her garage as I went off to college and later, the business world. It seemed only fitting that the same car should be my son's first. Maybe together we'd be able to get her back running again.

When I went to pick it up, I told my mother I was going to restore the broken down muscle car with Steven. She chuckled and wished me luck, echoing my doubt I had that he'd appreciate the gift he was getting.

Steven rushed past Denise and I as he threw open the front door. He stood on the steps, looking out into the distance.

"Where's…. where's the car?" He said, as if his eyes entirely missed the sight of the rusty +car sitting amongst the other cars we had in the driveway.

"Steven, it's right in front of you. It's my old Barracuda." I explained, eyeing his change in expression as he realized which car he'd be getting. "We're going to restore it together. This is a classic and when it's cleaned up it will look better than any car out there." I explained to my shocked son.

"This can't be happening!" His words were met with feet stamping hard on the deck overlooking the driveway, as his hands clenched. "You're not being serious, are you? Stop messing around, where's the real car?" He asked, as if he hoped a shiny new Mercedes with a big blue bow on top was going to appear at the end of our driveway. He turned, meeting his eyes with mine, full of disgust.

"He'll come around," Denise reassured me. She said this every time Steven had his "episodes," partially trying to convince me, but more to convince herself that there was more to our son than these awful moments. I had lost all hope, as I thought Steven might have seen the car and thought of it as a way to spend time with me restoring it.

The table was all set and I yelled up the stairs for Steven to come down. He plopped down in his seat, where I caught a glimpse of his swollen, tear filled eyes. Dinner proceeded quietly until I asked Steven if he would help me push the car into the garage for the night.

"It doesn't even run? Great dad, thanks," he snarled sarcastically back at me.

"Remember when you were younger and needed to build that toy car for your Boy Scouts Derby?" I asked him.

"Yeah I remember", Steven rudely retorted back.

"Well we worked all Saturday and whittled that thing out of wood, only for it to not drive straight." I enthusiastically pointed out.

"Then you two worked on it for hours to make sure it would win that Derby Trophy" Denise chimed in.

After a few moments of silently eating his potatoes, I heard a mumble of "Yeah sure I guess I'll help". My wife and I quickly exchanged looks of hope as we continued to eat dinner.

The two of us panted as we pushed the car into the garage. There Steven got to see the rust in its full beauty under our bright artificial lighting.

"Dad this thing's a piece of shit" Steven said with a chuckle.

"This was your old man's first car When he said these words, my hope had been fulfilled. I knew once he asked this, that I was going to have my son back.

"I would love to", I said with a smile. "First vacuum the interior and I'll figure out why she isn't running."

"Ew dad gross! There's like 10 years of dust in here" he complained.

I popped open the hood and began to investigate the source of the old girl not starting. Everything looked electronically sound, but fuel wasn't getting to all eight injectors. Further inspecting the feed and return lines, I discovered there was a crack in the feed line, leaving the injectors dryer than the Sahara. This was something we could tape up for now. There had to be something else wrong with the car.

I watched as Steven vacuumed out the interior of his new car, starting to remember how I'd done the same thing so many years ago, starting to believe that, maybe along with the car, our relationship was salvageable.

The next day in the garage I began to bond with my son.

"A car's fairly simple buddy," I explained. "All it needs to run is fuel, air, and power."

He stared at me blankly.

"Lets try and start her up and see if she has any of those." I said.

I threw Steven the keys which he fumbled with as he found the spot to insert them. He was only used to my "Push to Start" button in my Beamer.

The Barracuda began making a cranking sound as the aggressive headlights illuminated to life. This was a good sign- the car had electricity.

"This is pointless!" Steven exclaimed to me, noticeably frustrated.

"Hold on" I said as I fumbled for any sort of sprayable liquid.

I explained to Steven that if the car was getting electricity and air, all we needed was fuel.

"Spraying this brake cleaner in the intake should get the car running" I explained.

"You spray and I'll turn the key" He said.

I was really beginning to have faith in our little project. He turned the key and I sprayed the cleaner into the circular filter. The car quenched the refreshing cleaner and roared to life.

"It worked Dad!" he exclaimed as a big grin stretched across his once dissatisfied face.

Not more than two seconds later, the car stuttered and died.

"Wait what?", my no longer excited son mumbled.

"Oh good" I said with a sigh of relief. It was indeed a fuel issue. The old girl was running for a measly few seconds because she had no fuel to run off of. The fuel pump had to be busted.

"What do you mean good? I thought I was going to be able to take my drivers test in this car" Steven said in a yet again, spoiled manner.

"It's the fuel pump." I said to him. "Not a hard fix. I'm going to show you how to use a ratchet and a floor jack. The pump is inside of the fuel tank on these cars, meaning we have to remove the tank from the car. I'll order the pump, and we can work again when it comes in"

Unhappy that the car wasn't fixed, Steven walked inside.

Hey, at least we spent time together. I thought to myself.

Time passed as we waited for the pump to come in. Unfortunately I noticed Steven had begun to lose interest. Despite the fact that I told him it would take a few weeks to come in, he still checked outside the door everyday to see if it had come. This gave me a sense of hope in him, but boy I wish the part will come in before he gives up.

A few more days pass and the small box we had been waiting for arrived. He eagerly opened it as I watched over his shoulder. We then went into the garage where I showed him how to jack up the rear end of the car. Denise watched in utter fear that the car would fall on us, but I taught Steven how to properly secure it. After showing him how to use the ratchet, I told him the gas tank had to be unbolted and removed from the car.

"Loosen those four bolts holding up the fuel tank, then let me know and I'll help you with putting in the new pump." I said.

"Sounds good" He said I was so happy to hear the enthusiasm in his voice.

Denise opened the door and told me work had called and wanted me to come back in.

"What?!" Steven cried out when he heard the news. "We were just going to have her running", he said in utter disappointment.

"I showed you what to do," I reassured him, "Just take everything slow. I'll be back shortly."

It was 9:30 PM when I got back. Turning up the driveway, I saw the lights in the garage off. I sighed in utter disappointment. He needed me there to help him, but as usual, work got in the way.

A few years ago, I bought Steven the new Mario Kart for us to play. The long smirk that stretched across his face told me he wanted a challenge. I distinctly remember staying up late into the night, letting him beat me in every race. Those were our good times. I assumed he has lost hope or interest in the car due to me leaving. Small glimmers of hope began to flutter as I hoped he had still wanted to work on the car with me. I appreciated having a career that pays well, but it just may have sabotaged my last ditch effort to revive Steven.

I got inside and walked up our long stairs; headed towards Steven's room. I hesitantly knocked on his closed door.

"What do you want?", my snooty son snarled.

"Did you fix the car? What happened buddy?", I said in a peppy optimistic tone.

"What happened is you left me" he wisely retorted. "All I needed to do was put in the pump and we would have been done."

"I'm sorry." I said. Not knowing how else to respond.

I had let him down.

"Let's go put it in now" I said.

"You do realize it's like 11:30 and I have school in the morning right?"

Yet again, another snarky comment.

"You can take a day off" I chuckled.

"Hey no! He needs to go to school!" yelled my wife. But we were already down the stairs before she could catch us.

I guided him with installing the pump.

"Watch this" He said as he showed off his new skills of using a ratchet to re install the fuel tank.

I couldn't help but smile as I realized Steven was starting to enjoy working for things he wanted.

Dropping the hood down, he looked at me expectantly, waiting for the next step.

"That should be everything. Hop inside and start her up!" I almost yelled. The car took a few turns, before the v8 came roaring back to life. Denise came outside and walked over to me.

"I could recognize the sound of this car from anywhere. I still re-member the dates we went on in this thing."

"It's going to be a good car for him" I reassured her.

Stephen turned off the car and came running over to his mother and me with a smile plastered his face- something we hadn't seen in years.

Business as Usual

Wildwood- she sits proudly next to the murky Atlantic, where he dips his feet to cool off after long walks. On early mornings, he watches the burning sun cut through pale pink skies. Soft sands stretch endlessly, cushioning the mossy rocks on which he always scuffs his already dirty sandals.

He longs to spend the day lost in the jungle of sea shells and driftwood, but the Boardwalk beckons him to return. His feet pick up speed as he runs, leaping over the splintering ramp and landing safely on the wooden slats. Digging in his too small pockets for the key, he recognizes the scent of fresh bread and garlic wafting from the only bakery nearby. As his fingers fumble, he notices a small silver flash in the corner of his eye. The sight sends a bolt of adrenaline through his body as he jumps down to grab the coins below. *One, two, three, four, five quarters. One dollar and twenty-five cents.* Smiling, he jangles the change in his hand as he finally grabs hold of the small silver key from between the fabric folds. Eagerly, he unlocks the door and pushes it in, the handle already sweating in the humidity. His hand searches for the light switch, pushing aside a cobweb to flick it on.

The shop floor looks as if it hasn't been touched in years. Candy bars and chips are stacked neatly where they had been places months ago. Bottles of sunscreen and sunglasses sit patiently in the shelves. Yet, it's only been a day since he was standing in the same exact spot, opening the store once more. Ignoring the bleak nature of the store floor, he rushes behind the counter. Crouching down, he flings open the bottom-most drawer to reveal the bowl, which is now almost filled to the top with a mountain of coins. Lifting his hand, he drops the quarters into the bowl, reveling in the satisfying *clink clink* of each coin hitting the top of the pile. He takes a minute to observe his savings, noticing just how close the coins are to filling the bowl. Smiling, he closes the drawer and stands once more. *Almost there.* Sighing, he picks up the broom and sweeps mindlessly, preparing himself for another day of scrubbing down sticky counters and re-stocking cold sodas that only sat in the same refrigerator for months. His duties are so routine that he never thinks about the job before he jumps into action.

Suddenly, a stinging pain rips across his palm. His hand recoils in response, feeling the too-familiar bite of a popped callus. Clenching his fist to stop the bleeding, he sits behind the counter for a minute's rest.

The store has collected more dust than usual today. The grey cash register sits heavily on the otherwise empty countertop, its buttons half-broken. His palm, though still stinging, itches as he looks at the register once more.

Shifting in his seat, he takes a key out of his back pocket. Sliding it into the slot, he turns it clockwise until he hears the satisfying *pop*. As the drawer opens, he hesitantly slides it open, his head turning away so as to not be disappointed at the measly sight.

Inside, only a few wrinkled twenties lay surrounded by a cluster of pennies and nickels. Though he knew the situation was grave before, this only confirms his worst fear. As if he must be mistaken, he picks up the bills and begins to flip through them. *Twenty, forty, sixty, eighty. Eighty dollars and ten, twenty, thirty-three cents.*

He jumps, startled, as the door squeaks open. Quickly, he shoves the cash back into the drawer, slamming it shut as he leaps off of the stool and picks up the broom once more.

"Hey, kiddo!" he hears a voice call.

"Oh, hi Mom. I didn't know you'd get here so early," he says, resting the broom against the counter again.

"No earlier than usual, sweetie," she responds, walking towards him to leave a kiss on his forehead. "It's already ten o'clock. Any customers yet?" she asks, a hint of hope in her voice.

"No, not yet," he sighs. "But I swept up behind the counter," he points out, hoping to quell her disappointment.

"Thank you, love," she smiles, dropping her purse on the counter with a *thud*. He can't help but notice the dark, puffy circles sitting prominently underneath her eyes and her hair frizzing in every direction.

"Are you okay? You look exhausted," he comments, trying to fill the tired silence.

"Well, that's what happens when you have to work two jobs to keep one business afloat," she says, annoyed. "I don't really get the chance to sleep much, even on the graveyard shift."

Though she tidies the untouched mints on the shelf, her sharp movements show her irritation.

"Um, I'm sorry, Mom. I didn't mean to make you mad," he explains. He's interrupted, though, by the sound of the door heaving open once more.

"Hi, uh. Are you guys open?" he asks, poking his head slowly through the doorway.

Instantly, his mother snaps to attention. She reaches up to fix her hair and to smooth the wrinkles in her button down.

"Yes! Of course we're open!" she grins, gesturing for him to come inside.

"Oh, okay," he says, hesitantly entering the store. "I haven't seen one store open yet. I haven't even seen another person, actually. Business slow today?" he questions. As he enters, it becomes clear what kind of clientele he is. His khaki shorts and boat shoes are a sure sign that he's another rich New Yorker on a quick getaway. His mother's face, once plastered with a smile, now begins to revert back to its usual expression.

"Um, I suppose. If you count all of 2008 a slow day," she laughs pitifully. The customer lets out a forced chuckle as he walks around to the fridges in the back and pulls out a water.

"That's all?" his mother asks, hoping by some miracle he'll buy anything else.

"Yeah... you guys take credit cards?" he questions, pulling out his platinum card and flashing it in her direction.

"No, sorry. Cash only."

"Alright," he responds, irritation creeping into his voice. "Well, can you break a hundred?"

"Um…" she unlocks the cash drawer quickly and looks inside, only to find the four twenty dollar bills. "No. I'm so sorry," she says, her cheeks flushing red.

"A fifty?" he asks, now with eyebrows furling in disbelief. Without a word, she shakes her head no. "Hmph," he sighs, slamming the water down on the counter and tossing the cash back into his wallet. As he begins to walk back towards the door, his mother calls out in a last attempt to save the sale; but, he's already gone, leaving the door half open as he stomps out of the store.

"Sorry, Mom," he says quietly, watching her eyes swelling with tears.

"Don't be, honey," she sighs, rubbing his back to comfort him. "Hey, you've been here all morning. You wanna take your break?" she asks, hoping to cheer him up.

"No, no. You should go home and sleep. I can take the store for another day," he assures.

"No, please. I need an hour to tidy, love. You know how I get," she smiles and laughs, grabbing a tissue off the counter to dab at her eyes.

"You sure?" he questions again.

"Positive," she says, planting a small kiss on the top of his head.

"Okay. If you're sure," he smiles, heading towards the door. "I'll be back soon, though!" he calls over his shoulder as he exits and shuts the door softly behind him.

As he steps out onto the briny wood of the Boardwalk, the wave of salty sea air that smacks him in the face is a welcomed relief from the stagnant air of the store. He places his hand on the wooden railing as he starts to stroll, having no place to be and no money to spend.

Even though it is a sunny Friday afternoon, the Boardwalk is sparse. The usual crowds of teenagers and stressed out families on vacation are a distant memory. As he looks at the empty stores stretching for miles in front of him, the only faces he sees are the ones his eyes create in the abstract swirls of fog in the distance.

On his left, he notices the t-shirt shop's racks of clearance clothing outside. The sign on the rack reads "All items must go. Going out of business sale." Nervously, he picks up the pace and continues shuffling along.

He can remember a time where he would walk down a Boardwalk congested with so many people that their faces were a blur of color and expression. They'd stand in their bathing suits and Hawaiian shirts, faces slathered in sunscreen and sunglasses perched on their heads. Children ran gleefully with life-sized stuffed animals in their hands, arcade tokens spilling out their pockets, and smiles plastered to their faces. The salty air would buzz with conversation and excitement, unlike the stagnant air that hung heavily in the air now.

His thoughts are cut short by a flash of silver in between the wooden slats below him. In an instant, he crouches to look at the treasures below. *Five quarters, two nickels, and six dimes. One dollar and ninety-five cents.* He grabs the change, cradling the dirt encrusted coins in his palm as if he's holding a newborn. His thumb runs over the faces, tracing their edges delicately. As he jangles their weight in his hand, he musters a half-smile as he reaches to put them in his pocket. His knees unlock as he stands and his heavy feet begin their slow trudge back to the store.

Though he has just walked this way no more than ten minutes ago, he's dreading this trip even more. Seeing the failed businesses and bankrupt shops only makes him more unsettled than usual. He tries to keep his eyes down at his feet, but a glimmer of a neon sign pulls his eye to the right. In the dirty window hangs a simple red and blue 'Open" sign half-covered by old-fashioned lace curtains. He blinks as if he cannot believe what he's seeing; but, when he does, the candy shop is still standing there. His hand reaches back into his pocket to pull out the fistful of change. As he stands in front of the store door, he looks back down at the money in his palm. The weight of the change feels so heavy to him that he can almost feel his arm fall to the floor. *Alright. Just go home now and add it to the bowl.* He could practically hear the metal sound of the change hitting the top of the pile. *You need every cent more than ever now!* Images of the measly bills in the drawer ran rampant through his mind. *But just one dollar and ninety-five cents. Would that really make a difference?* Now hypnotised by the sign, he shakes his head and pushes through the sticking door, his curiosity overriding everything else.

As soon as he enters, the sickeningly sweet odor hits his face. On

229

the rightmost wall are shelves of neat, glass jars, filled to their tops with penny candy. His pensive look melts as he runs over, his eyes widening at the sight; but, as his excited eyes drift towards the prices on the small cards standing next to the jars, his smile fades. *A dollar fifty. Seventy-five cents. Three dollars per piece.* Just thinking about spending more than a dollar causes him to break out in a cold sweat. His eyes continue down the line of prices until he comes across one he can manage. *Twelve cents per piece.* Behind the sign is a tall jar packed with salt water taffy. Eagerly, he pulls off the heavy lid and digs his hand inside. Though he pulls out ten candies in his tight grip, he drops six as he calculates the cost in his mind. *Forty-eight cents. Doable.*

As he heads towards the register, he notices the side eye from the young blonde cashier who is chewing her gum at a deafening volume. In between her scrunched shoulder and neck, she balances her cell phone.

"Hey, I gotta go," she says into the phone, motioning him closer towards the register. Hesitantly, he steps forward and drops the candies on the counter. Through the phone, he can hear a voice screech a high pitched 'What?''.

"I said I gotta go!" she yells back, her hands flying up in frustration. "I got a customer for like, the first time in forever. Be right back," she explains, slamming the phone back down. "Sorry about that," she smiles, though there's an edge of sarcasm in her voice. As she glances down at the pitiful candies, a puzzled look crosses her face. "That's all?" she questions, with another smug look.

"Uh, yeah," he says, placing two quarters in front of her. Slowly, she picks up the coins and pops open the drawer. To fill the silence, he clears his throat awkwardly. "So… have you guys had a lot of business, uh, lately? I haven't seen many stores open today…" he trails off.

"Um, I mean, not really. I only work here during the nice weather though. It's my parents' summer project, ya know," she says, shrugging nonchalantly. "They wanted to teach me responsibility or something like that. I don't really know," she chuckles. He lets out a laugh, but her words sting in his sore mind. He can't help but notice the flashy bracelets and silver rings decorating her hands and wrists. As she drops the coins into the drawer, her face crumples into a confused squint.

"Do you have any pennies? I'm out," she explains. He looks down as if more change will suddenly appear in his hand, but eventually squeaks out a 'no'.

"Ugh, I'll have to go in the back," she whines, rolling her eyes. "Is it okay if you just don't get the two pennies? Take it as a tip, sort of?" she asks, her flipping her hair back and raising her eyebrows in hopes of charming her way out of her work.

"Um, I actually could really use those pennies today," he mutters, careful not to make eye contact with her judgeful glare.

"Alright," she sighs. "Be right back."

As she bolts into the back room of the store, she leaves the register wide open. His curious eyes can't help but to peek into the cash drawer that has been left ajar. Though he expects to see a couple of fifties, maybe even a hundred dollar bill, he is shocked by what he sees lying inside.

The drawer is bursting with cash. Thick stacks of fifty and one hundred dollar bills stuff the too small compartments. He can feel his fast heartbeat speed up as his hands tense up with awe. Turning back to look at the girl in the back room, he sees her hands flying as she digs through old boxes and bags in search of the penny rolls. His head snaps back to the sight of the open register, sitting defenseless on the counter. Instantly, his hand shoots out to snatch five, crisp hundred dollar bills off the top of the pile. The sound of the girl's footsteps suddenly grow closer, making him jump. Anticipating her response, his shoulders tense up involuntarily.

"Okay, here. Two pennies," she says, reaching out to place them in his now open palm. There he stands, frozen in place, as she shuts the register drawer and picks up her phone again. "Here, here. You're all set," she mutters, pushing the candies toward him hurriedly. Still in a trance, he scoops them up and places them in his pocket as he exits the store, checking behind him nervously.

Closing the door behind him, he takes a deep breath as he recollects his thoughts. His stomach is in knots; a mix of adrenaline, excitement, and a sudden overwhelming feeling of guilt gather in his chest as he picks up his tired feet and heads back towards the store, trying to quell the anxious thoughts in his mind.

She didn't really need that money. Did you see the stacks of bills in that drawer? She's wearing my entire family fortune on her wrist. She won't miss two measly hundreds. Though he tries to rationalize his actions, he can't extinguish the burning guilt inside. He barely realizes he's back to the store by the time he's standing not more than two feet away.

Alright, you gotta go in. He stands with one hand on the doorknob, waiting for a wave of courage to push it in. *She'll understand. She'll be happy even. Think of what two hundred dollars can do.* With this thought planted in his mind, he finally pushes the door open.

"Hey Mom! I'm back," he calls. From the office, her head pops out with a tired smile to say hello.

"Hey, love," she shouts, noticing the odd look on his face. "What's up? You look worried," she comments.

"Nothing," he says quickly, walking over to join her in the office; but, he soon changes his mind. "Well, I think I got something. Something that could help us out a little bit," he mutters. Hearing this, her face brightens up.

"Really, honey? Whaddya mean?" she asks, intrigued. He reaches into his back pocket to pull out the five bills and to place them in her hand. Instantly, her eyebrows raise in surprise.

"What? Where did you get this, honey? You didn't sell anything, did you?" she questions in disbelief.

"No, mom," he chuckles. "What do I have to sell, anyways. I... I took it from that candy store. From down the Boardwalk."

Instantly, her face of happy shock changes to a face of anger. "You're saying you stole this money?" she whispers, unable to raise her now quivering voice.

"No, no," he tries to explain. "I didn't really steal it. You should've seen the money in that place, Mom. The girl said it's just her parents' summer project. She didn't even know it was missing, I promise," he justifies. Still, she can't seem to say a word. *Why is she being this way? Isn't she happy we'll have rent for another month? Who cares how I got it?*

"I just knew we could really use it. I thought maybe we could avoid the bus for a while? Maybe get the car fixed..." he suggests. A queasy feeling washes over him as he watches involuntary tears well in the corners of his mother's fluttering eyes. Her lower lip trembles while a salty tear creeps down his cheek and makes its way into the corner of his frown.

"I'm sorry, Mom," he cries. He can't help but to think of the only money left in the drawer again.

"It's just that I saw the register this morning. Business is slow, Mom. I know it is," he explains. Still, she says nothing. "I'm here all morning and all night. And no matter how many times I sweep up or organize or do anything to help the store, no one ever comes."

He pauses as he looks pensively around the store, noticing every item still sitting stagnantly in its original spot. "And… I know that we're running out of money. You can't keep that from me forever."

He reaches back into his pocket and, this time, grabs hold of the register key with ease. He unlocks the drawer to remove the four bills, but only finds two resting inside. *One, two. Forty dollars.* With a puzzled expression, he cranes up his neck to look back at his mother. "Is - is this all that's left?" he asks, praying that there's some mistake.

Silently, but solemnly, she nods. In disbelief, he lets out a gasp as he looks back at the money resting in his palm. "Why didn't you tell me?" he demands. "Why have you been acting like we're all fine when we aren't?"

"I didn't want you to have to worry, love. You shouldn't have to worry. We'll be fine, I promise," she says, hoping to calm him down.

"We're not fine!" he exclaims. "I'm tired of acting like we are! And I'm tired of walking everywhere because we have no car, and I'm tired you always being at work, and I'm tired of running this store all by myself!" he screams, crossing his arms to show his frustration.

"Love, please. Please calm down," she begs, holding her head in her hands.

"And now you're mad that I 'stole' something. I'm just trying to keep us going for another month. Can't you see that?" he argues.

"It was wrong, love. You cannot break the law, no matter what circumstances there are!" she argues back, now growing angry. "Yes, I tried to keep this from you. A fifteen year old shouldn't have these worries!" she yells, throwing up her hands. "If that makes me a bad mother, then fine. But I didn't know I was a bad enough mother to raise a thief," she says, shaking her head heatedly.

Before she has time to say anything more, he runs out of the office and slams the door behind him. At the front of the store, he's left in the uncomfortable silence, alone with his racing mind. *Was I too harsh on her?* He fidgets with the keys in his pocket. *No. She's being unreasonable.* His fists ball up in anger again. *But... she was just trying to protect me, wasn't she? So I wouldn't have to worry more than I already am.* The only feeling he has now is the sting of guilt and disappointment clawing at him inside. Suddenly, his intense expression begins to melt into a pensive stare.

Alright, alright. So I'll bring the money back later. He sighs disappointedly as he takes a last look at the waxy bills in his fingers. *But rent. There's no way we can make it through the end of the month on forty dollars.* He returns to the register to put away the rest of the money, but as he shuts the drawer, he can't help but to notice a flash of silver below him.

Suddenly, the pieces begin to fall together. Bending down, he reaches the bottom-most drawer and grabs the rusted over handle to slide it open. Inside, the metal bowl sits, almost full with change. In the reflection of the glimmering coins, he can see every penny he's saved for so long sitting inside. *Well, I guess this is it. Goodbye bike. Goodbye car.* Though it pains him, he understands what he has to do.

He picks it up, cradling its heft in the crook of his arm, before standing again. With a grunt, he carries the bowl to his mother's now closed door. Quietly, he pushes the small door open and sets down the bowl with a thud.

"I'm sorry."

Through Different Eyes
Authors and Illustrators

Alumni Author Selection
Find a Penny, Pick it Up...

My edges have worn down a great deal over time - it has been over fifty years since I was conceived. My name is Abraham Lincoln, I'm a 1960 edition, born and raised in West Point, New York. I'm close to worthless; in fact, my net worth is that of a cent. A single cent. I have had the honor of traveling this lovely nation - seeing countless wallets, a multitude of back pockets, and thousands of coin trays. I have heard marriage proposals, break ups, joyous news being delivered, and people trying to sing along with trendy pop tunes.

Amongst these things, I have also had the pleasure of knowing several types of people: pompous athletes, quiet students, bubbly children, and miserable office workers. These classes of people may seem as if they cannot possibly have a thing in common; yet, they are all people. Human beings that continuously ignore my worth. How would you feel if someone saw you, sitting there, helpless on the ground, and they simply ignored you? Terrible. Absolutely terrible. Rotten. It's horrid I tell you. Everyone else that's like me is loved - even the nickels and dimes are shown affection. Vending machines readily accept my cousins and uncles and aunts. They spit me back out - as if I'm worthless.

Am I?

Mathematically, no. I possess some form of monetary value; basic arithmetic dictates that because I'm worth more than zero, even by a slight amount, I am worth something. So, for Christ's sake, treat me as if I'm useful!

When I was just a mere infant, my life had so much purpose. Small children would dive into busy streets to snatch me up; often times they would push one another and pull hair. Once, a little girl was slugged in the face by her not-so-lovely older sister, in an attempt to purchase a wrapped candy. After bravely warding off any potential looters, the older sister hopped down the cracked asphalt of the street. Her palms were clammy and her nails were bitten down to stubs; I could still hear her little sister wailing on the curb, demanding that I be brought back. When have you ever been fought over by two girls? As she continued her quest to the Mecca of candy, I caught glimpses of the brilliant blue hues of the sky and felt the warmth of the sun on my engravings. Life is good. Heck, they even named the candy after me! The number of days I spent in sweet smelling candy shops was overwhelming - the nostalgic feeling that it incites is blissful.

I can vividly recall being comfortably situated against the manila-hued wall of the cash register. Its cool sides brought support to my lower ridges and I conversed with long lost family members. We'd chat about all different types of things - my Aunt Sue was a rambler.

She would go on and on and on, criticizing me for having a strangely printed head as if this was somehow my fault. One night I nearly had enough.

"Abe, why don't we just get you smelted back to normal, Hun?" She questioned.

"'Cause this is how I was born, this is how I'm gonna stay." I retorted. What did she know about how pennies were supposed to look anyways?

Some days, no one would touch me. The radio would spit out a panicked voice of a young male and people would frantically scatter about - I longed for their touch. They were too busy running home to their families to worry about little old me, though.

One of the longest periods of isolation I faced was when a teenaged girl placed me in the tip jar at a gas station - the man on the radio began blabbing once more over some important guy with the last name "Ken" being shot. The shop went dark for a few days - no one came in, no one bothered to fight over me, no one bothered to even just flip me around for a bit. Let's not forget - the face engraved on me, you know, the Abraham Lincoln was also shot. Whoop-dee-doo.

Thankfully, I became valued once more and business was booming. By my tenth birthday, I had begun to develop a greenish tint around my edges. Yep, that's right, I was becoming a man.

The whole attitude in America had also begun to shift; I started to witness people claiming money is obsolete and "love is all you need." I ended up laying in countless fields and spent much more time in the coin trays of beat up vans - it was okay. Granted, I missed the high-energy buzz of the candy shops, but people were just so incredibly calm. I dug it. I needed a break, I deserved a break! I was only ten and quite dull - I didn't want to see all of my shininess disappear before I reached 20. I blame my dullness on the stress my admirers put on me.

I'm basically a therapist, you should hear some of the things people tell pennies. Christ, this one girl - Anne was her name - she found me laying face up at some concert... "Stocks of Wood" or something.... Sheesh, you humans can be weird...Anyways, Anne was a sweetheart. She found me, scooped me up ever so gently, and prayed to God that her day would be lucky. Two hours later her boyfriend proposed - Anne kept me for nearly a year. I sat on her nightstand next to a lamp, a pile of records, and some herbs that she called "grass." Normally, I would have complained about not being out and about. However, life on the nightstand was relaxing.

There was no real concept of time with Anne and her husband, Mark. They seemed to get up when they pleased and lounge around for long periods of time. The two were never in a rush and generally happy, though the room was often times quite smoky. My eyes would water and I'd begin to wheeze. But hey, who am I to complain, they kept me safe. I was beginning to notice that I was much more stationary. This forced me to pay more attention to the couple than I normally would have. I became attached.

One day, on a rainy Saturday afternoon, Mark received a letter in the mail demanding his presence at the town hall auditorium on the following Monday. The weekend was much more emotional than usual - Anne seemed heartbroken but I couldn't figure out why. Mark promised he'd be safe and that he'd write her every day...A handful of months went by and Anne received another letter. Mark never came home. She cried for hours, rifling through his drawers and burying her face in his old clothes. Then she rummaged through the closet, tearing apart old boxes filled with pictures and treasured mementos; she was hysterical. Finally, Anne collapsed on the bed - where she saw me, still on the night stand. She picked me up, opened the front door, and threw me into the street.

"Some luck you gave me" She screamed as I flew through the air.

"Anne!" I wanted to yell so badly. I wanted to scream at the top of my engraving and apologize - I knew I hadn't done anything wrong; I just wanted her to keep me.

I was not accustomed to this. People never just tossed me out! People always wanted me.

From there, it was downhill. The streets never felt so cold, I never felt so alone. People would occasionally stroll by, sometimes picking me up and muttering, "Find a penny pick it up, all day long you'll have good luck." Oh, how I wished I could spit on them. I am not lucky; I am a federally issued piece of legal tender!

I was, at this point, extremely faded and crusty - I almost didn't blame people for not picking me up half the time. I was an outcast. But, I was not the only one - occasionally guys would pick me up and toss me about for a few minutes. After becoming bored, they'd put me back on the ground; a child would then go to pick me up afterward and their mothers would scold them for even giving me a second look. Not every child was so obedient, though. Chuck, a little blonde haired, blue -eyed toddler gracefully scooped me up after a flamboyant clerk flicked me to the ground. His mother immediately became hysterical, screaming to the surrounding customers about how "the faggots were running wild... they were out to infect us....didn't anyone see how carelessly he tossed that penny to the ground for someone else to pick up..." I wasn't quite sure what that meant but it just didn't seem nice, especially since they always talked with one another, warning them about AIDing people. Everyone deserves love, don't they?

This continued for quite some time; people began to adopt the universal precaution mindset. I was a penny. They didn't know where I had been, who had touched me, or what was on me - so, they simply avoided me at all costs. You would have thought that touching me was a death sentence with some of the reactions I got. The neglectful attitudes expressed towards my worth began to take a toll on me; I became extremely dull.

I guess you could say life slowly got better. Soon people were running these incredible machines that whizzed and flickered lights right from their own homes. The Calvin family had one of the most impressive set-ups I had ever seen; their young daughter Tessa was trying to save up for a new radio of some sort and began to collect change on the coffee table. From the table I could see two boxes that screeched fascinating noises and shone bright lights; one of them played music nonstop. The kids called it "NTV" or something. The other machine was strictly for their mother's use. After she came home from work, she'd sit at a desk in front of it and frantically hit the buttons on a board beneath it. I later learned that this was a computer and she was typing.

The Calvins were an average, middle-class, suburban family. Nothing exciting ever really happened; every now and then someone would start an argument...Mrs. Calvin would snip at her husband, "Have you ever heard of napkins, dearest?"

"Oh, why yes I have!" He replied back.

"Well?"

"Well, what my love?" Mr. Calvin would murmur as he picked up a pile of napkins, only to toss them on the floor.

It was painful to listen to and even harder to watch, but one could tell deep down that the two truly did care for one another.

As more and more time passed, Tessa forgot about her quest to save up for her radio - I slid around on the smooth polished grain of the table, sometimes so much that I would become nauseous. Then, it happened. Rex, the family's abomination of a pet, decided that it'd be a great idea to lick me. He must have enjoyed my taste because then the mutt granted me the pleasure of touring his gastrointestinal tract. Someone most likely realized that their beloved pooch was sick and, before I knew it, I was in the gloved hands of a masked figure that reeked of antiseptic.

One may think that experiencing the inside of a dog's bowels would be terrible; however, it is what the surgeon said to his nurse that really got to me. After he carefully extracted me from Rex's stomach, the nurse shot him a look and asked what to do with me.

The doctor simply replied, "Toss it."

That's right; they just tossed me amidst hundreds of used latex gloves and syringes. From there, a biohazard waste truck came and took me away. There was a special dump for "trash" like us. It was filled with mountains of needles, gauze, and objects that had been exposed to various bodily fluids - the dump was miserable. I longed for Anne, I wanted out. I even missed my crazy Aunt Sue.

Telling time became even more difficult - I couldn't eavesdrop as I had previously done, nor could I peek at the newspaper thrown on the sofa. Instead, I would have to wait, and wait, and wait for some clipping of an article or ad to make its way to the dump. The years dragged on - days became painful and the weeks became dreary. Having my head flipped around let me see things in a different light, I guess.

I mean, there were others like me in the piles of trash; yet, the way that their heads faced made it impossible for them to even glance at the few intriguing things present. I was thankful for my deformity.

Though living through absolute hell for close to five years was slightly traumatic, the most terrifying day of my life occurred when I sat outside of a local supermarket. A seagull scooped up a small prescription box I was in at the dump and carried me over several parking lots. The stupid bird took a hard left and bam. I was on the ground. It was probably close to 2005. The soft gray hues of the sky melted into the horizon as rain drops pooled close to the curb, where I sat. I was face down.

With each individual drop, I could feel the pool around me begin to grow. Soon, it passed my ridges, the water continued to slowly creep up. I cursed the seagull who had let me slip from his beak.

Hours passed and the small pool transformed into a lake - I had no choice but to suffer through it. I couldn't help but blame my misfortune on the manner in which I landed; tails up. People continuously walked by me - some stopped for a brief moment, glancing quickly - only to recoil once they saw that I was, in fact, heads down. Is the mere orientation of my body enough to send small children and housewives running for the hills? Apparently, it was.

Eventually, the rain ceased. The sun began to shine once more. I was so tired, my engravings ached, and my mind was just worn out. While the weather improved my outlook remained stagnant.

I am worth something. Why don't they see it, I'd question myself. So many kids would walk by without even noticing me. I used to be fought over. I used to be treasured, I used to be lucky. I am worth something.

Then, as if it was by the grace of God Himself, a strange man peeled me off the asphalt. His white t-shirt was littered with stains and he reeked of onions - it was close to putrid. I almost missed the dump when he brought me closer to his face. He wore wire-framed glasses that did anything but compliment his facial structure - and oh God, someone really needed to tell whoever he lived with to get him a nose hair trimmer. Maybe that was a bit too pretentious, I just wanted some company. I gave him a shot, not that I had a choice.

I later learned that his name was Phil, that he had a strange liking of pickles for breakfast, and that for decades everyone that walked past me was missing out. You see, Phil was a coin collector and was the only person to ever realize that I am a misprint. Yes, you heard me. I really am worth something - well, a lot more than just something. I now sit peacefully on a shelf with others of my kind. Every now and then we get taken down for a dusting and an occasional cleaning; Phil is a strange, strange man, but he's the only person to devote his/her life to me.

Sitting there, helpless on the shelf, I let my mind wander. I began to delve into the hypocrisy behind my conception. No, it wasn't one of an immaculate sort - the government demanded that I be put into use; they claimed I was needed. They claimed that the dollar stores of America desperately needed me - yet, they failed to mention that it cost nearly double my net worth to create me - 2.7 cents.

Sadly, many of my cousins and distant relatives aren't as fortunate as me - they can't coast off of a mindless mistake. They are forced to live a miserable life filled with nonchalant glances and dirty coin trays. Rarely will someone treasure their worth. Knowing this, it's incredibly hard for me to favor the production of thousands more of our kind. Recalling what rock bottom felt like still causes twinges of pain beneath my copper surface, it's enough to make my face scrunch up and my edges to writhe. The world is a cruel place for a penny, especially when the only attention you really get is based off a flaw. We're still money; people just seem to forget that we are actually worth something.

Now that doesn't make much sense, does it?